DATE DUE

HOSTAGE IN A HOSTAGE WORLD

Hope Aboard
Hijacked TWA 847

B. Christian Zimmermann

Publishing House
St. Louis

Chapter 6, pages 65–81, is based on material from *How to Respond to Islam* by Philip H. Lochhaas. Copyright © 1981 by Concordia Publishing House.

Copyright © 1985 Concordia Publishing House
3558 S. Jefferson Avenue, St. Louis, MO 63118-3968
Manufactured in the United States of America

Library of Congress Cataloging-in-Publication Data

Zimmermann, B. Christian.
    Hostage in a hostage world.

        1. Hijacking of aircraft—United States—Case studies. 2. Christian life—1960-   . 3. Missions to Muslims. I. Title.
HE9803.Z7H59 1985   364.1'54   85-24269
ISBN 0-570-03998-3 (pbk.)

---

1 2 3 4 5 6 7 8 9 10 PP 94 93 92 91 90 89 88 87 86 85

To my loves:
Melvia, my wife,
Kaliki, Kéké, Kahalé, my children,
the memory of my parents and, especially, the Lord
Jesus, in whom they trusted

Contents

Foreword

In this book, one man—Christian Zimmermann—reflects on his experiences as a pastor-pilot-hostage on TWA Flight 847, from June 14, 1985, through his July 4 homecoming.

Zimmermann pulls together many details, some available elsewhere, some available only from his personal recollections. But Zimmermann does more than retell events. He adds his insight as a pastor and a Christian, and it helps us find meaning and hope in an otherwise senseless, tragic event.

The story told here is Zimmermann's. Undoubtedly, many of the events and emotions Zimmerman recalls mirror those of the other 38 hostages—perhaps even of all original 151.

No one book can compile a complete report from all 151 people, plus from Washington, D.C., Beirut, Algiers, Damascus, Jerusalem, Moscow, Tehran, and anywhere else tangentially involved.

Yet some statement can be made; some description given that is more complete than what is possible in a daily or weekly newspaper, magazine, radio, or television report; some description of Islam provided; and some vision of God's loving providence shared. If God loved us so much that He gave His one and only Son, then how could He allow the evil of this hijacking—or any evil for that matter—to explode into the world? And, why doesn't He do something about the other seven American hostages held somewhere in Lebanon?

Zimmermann's story offers one pastor-pilot-hostage's response.

As much as possible, this book is historically accurate. Information concerning the sequence of events has been gathered from Zimmermann's flight log as well as from his memory. To the fullest extent possible, the details as reported in the various media have been checked and rechecked. Many of these details can be found in appendix B: "Sequence of Events."

Some details will appear inaccurate because of the way people "put things together." For example, were there 39 or 40 remaining hostages? It depends on whether one includes the 40th person, James Palmer, Sr., of Little Rock, Ark, who was released only a few days earlier than the rest because of health problems.

Readers may ask whether a book like this should be written: "Does publicity about the hijacking, whether in the newspapers, news magazines, or a book, inadvertently support the hijackers' goal for publicity and encourage further terrorism? Wouldn't a total news blockade be better?" Zimmermann responds:

"No; I think that would have made the hijackers that much more desperate. True, the basics of their demands were publicized, but at the same time, the world viewed where they were coming from as being very cruel. [Besides,] how could anyone enforce a total, world-wide news blackout? Somebody would release the message and [the blackout] would be ineffective."

The Spelling of Arabic Words

Transliterating names and words from one language with its own alphabet into another language with a different alphabet poses many difficulties. There are no standards in English for transliterating from Arabic. For example, the Arabic name for the "Party of God" faction of the Shi'ites has been spelled as "Hesbollah" in London's *Daily Telegraph;* "Hezballah" in a suburban Chicago daily; "Hizballah" in *Time* magazine; "Hizbullah" in *Newsweek;* and "Hezbollah" in *The Daily Star,* an English newspaper in Beirut. We chose to use the last spelling.

We have kept the mark ' indicating the Arabic letter *'ayn* in the spelling of Shi'ite. But because it is more familiar to the reading public, we have used the anglicized ending *-ite* rather than following the Arabic spelling of the word as *Shi'a.*

Words that can be easily recognized and pronounced in English when closely transliterated have been kept as close to their Arabic origin as possible: *Qur'an, Muslim, Muhammad, Amal, Ayatollah, Jihad, Druze,* and *Sunni.*

Acknowledgments

Both author and publisher acknowledge the contributions of those involved in helping this book become a reality.

Perhaps the most important are the various media across the world who have helped, sometimes without their knowledge, in reconstructing the events that took place during the hijacking: Reuters: Associated Press; Universal Press Syndicate; United Press International; *The Chicago Tribune; The St. Louis Post-Dispatch; The Daily Star* of Beirut; *The Daily Telegraph* of London; *The Lutheran Witness;* The Lutheran Church—Missouri Synod, Board for Communication Services; *Time; Newsweek; U.S. News and World Report* and various other news services, as well as the photographers as noted in the credit lines to the photographs in this book. Although the story is Zimmermann's, all these have helped keep it accurate. To them all we express our thanks.

The Publisher

1.

Hostage!

Flight 847 began like any other flight. Our "weight slip" showed that we were about three-quarters full; but, because of a canceled flight to New York, some people had chosen to fly with us to Rome and transfer there to a New York–bound flight. At the last minute we ended up with every seat full: 145 passengers, five flight attendants (four, plus Mrs. Uli Derickson as purser), and three pilots—John Testrake as the captain, Phil Maresca as the co-pilot, and myself as the flight engineer.

Uli Derickson and I greeted the passengers as they came up the stairs. One girl said that she hated to leave Greece. I asked if she'd been on vacation. "Oh, yes," she said, "two glorious weeks on the beach. I'd much rather be there than going home." I didn't notice anything unusual about anybody; they were just a typical group of tourists.

We finally got under way shortly before 10 a.m. local time, and everything was still normal.

Fifteen minutes later, after we were airborne and well into the climb, we in the cockpit heard a commotion in the back—a lot of jumping around, someone shouting, "Oh, no!" and some banging.

Some noise isn't uncommon. When the flight attendants in the forward jump seats stand up, the seats automatically snap up to a stowed position and make a banging noise. Also, if one of the carrier door latches that hold the food carts comes loose during a climb, the carts roll out, causing a great amount of crashing and banging. That's what the noise sounded like.

But then it kept on. And there were a lot of other noises—pounding on the door, shouting, and the hostess call-button ringing furiously in the cockpit. Things no longer sounded normal.

Since I was sitting closest to the door, I looked through the peephole. I saw a gun very clearly and a man with a grenade in his hand.

Hijack!

What Now?

I considered the alternatives. All sorts of people had given us pilots all sorts of good advice, procedures to follow, things to do and not to do. But at this point the hijackers were kicking very hard on the door to get into the cockpit. Looking through the peephole, I could see they were trying to figure out the best angle from which to shoot off the door latch. "That's all we need," I thought, "someone shooting through the door into the cockpit!" So I told Testrake and Maresca that we were being hijacked.

Surprisingly, I didn't feel any unusual emotions at that point. Perhaps I was too busy to feel much of anything. I started thinking about what I had to do in this situation. It was a matter of thinking on our feet and drawing on a lot of previously assimilated training. I know our adrenaline started building.

I got back into my seat, strapped myself in, and asked John and Phil, "Okay, are you ready? Well, here we go." And I opened the door.

The hijackers burst in yelling, "This is a hijack! This is a hijack!" and immediately started pistol-whipping us.

They could have just walked in, pointed the pistol, and told us where they wanted to go. Instead, they were really savage. Perhaps they felt that they had to physically abuse the crew in order to gain control of the plane. They started banging around on all three of us. The first couple of times they tried pounding and even kicking Phil—which proved to be difficult in the close quarters of the cockpit.

Ultimately they found it was much easier to pound on me because I was closest to the door.

Each time they went in and out of the cockpit for perhaps the first half-dozen times (for about an hour), they would pound on me. They usually pounded on my shoulders with the butt of the gun. Most of it I bore fairly well—except when they cracked me on the back of the skull a couple of times. Then I saw stars. But I also survived that.

We were, however, very scared. We saw the grenade with the pin pulled, and we knew we were over the open waters of the Mediterranean. We had heard about suicide missions. And as soon as they started beating on us and yelling, we wondered, "How crazy are they? What are their intentions?"

When we finally caught the word *Algiers,* they didn't understand our response, "Okay, we'll go to Algiers." We started getting out maps and talking with each other about how to comply, but their immediate response was, "Don't talk! We go to Algiers! No talking!" But we needed to talk in order to plot our direction, check wind direction and strength, check whether we had enough fuel, and make other flight changes. That's a frustrating process if you can't talk.

Plus, while we had to comply with their demands, we also tried to figure out how we could gain control of the situation. In the meantime, we had to handle it their way.

We quickly realized we couldn't do it their way. We didn't have enough fuel to go to Algiers. We had to fill up somewhere else first. This too caused us a great deal of anxiety because they didn't understand what we were saying. We said "fuel," "gas," and "petrol," but nothing clicked. Finally, Uli found she could communicate with one of the hijackers in German—and that they referred to fuel as *benzin.*

We assured the hijackers that if we filled up with "benzin" wherever they wanted, then we could fly them to Algiers. With our suggestion, they decided on Beirut. We then settled into a routine that seemed acceptable to them, with the exception that we couldn't talk, either with each other or on the radio.

It wasn't trouble-free, however. The pain from the beatings, the possibility of more beatings, and our concern for the passengers forced us to remind ourselves continually that we had to keep up with the airplane. The 727 is not fully computerized, so pilots have a lot of things to do. It was easy to become distracted by the presence of the hijackers. On the other hand, working with the airplane kept our minds busy with the job at hand rather than fretting about the situation.

As I think back, I am thankful to the Lord that the cockpit door had a tendency to swing shut. I tried to keep it open so that the hijackers wouldn't get suspicious and start jumping around again, but nothing worked. So, first they kicked out a vent on the bottom of the door, evidently to use the opening as a space through which they could threaten us or throw a grenade. Then one of the hijackers used the vent to beat on the door knob until he broke off the entire assembly, leaving just a hole. I think he spent 10 minutes whacking away at that thing. It was a good outlet for his frustrations. At least it was better than beating away on one of us or on one of the passengers or flight attendants. It was just one more little thing that the Lord took care of.

The Need to Survive

We didn't calm down much on the way to Beirut, but we did have time to pray. It was a matter saying, "Okay, Lord, I've depended upon You for lots of little things. Now I've got to depend on You to work things out as we go on from here."

I knew the plane well and almost subconsciously did my job while I consciously tried to think of ways out of the problem. "Lord Jesus, give me some ideas; or at least lead me in the right direction." The prayer isn't much different from what all Christian pray as they conduct their normal business affairs—except that more was at stake.

By praying constantly and putting everything in the hands of God, my anxiety didn't show much. I was shaking inside, but I could look at myself and not see any shaking on the outside. It was a curious sensation to say, "Scared—I feel scared; but we just keep moving along. Things are just . . . happening. But nobody's been shot yet. They haven't released the trigger on the grenade yet. We're moving along. Yet I wish I didn't feel quite so shaky on the inside." Somehow, the more I had to operate the equipment, the more my mind was off the possibility of it all blowing up in my face.

About the time we flew past Cyprus, we came into radio contact with Beirut, which did not want us to land. We told Beirut that we didn't want to land there either, but we were being forced to land, and we *would* land—and, in fact, all we needed was fuel because the hijackers' intentions were not to come to Lebanon but to go to Algeria.

Finally Beirut was convinced and cleared us. The landing was normal. We taxied around onto a parallel taxiway. There the hijackers became extremely nervous. They did not want us to taxi any further, although a "Follow-Me" truck came toward us to lead us to the fuel area. But the truck stayed away because the hijackers were hanging out the window and waving their pistols around.

Following a great deal of radio talk with the tower, they worked out some kind of agreement, and we followed the vehicle into the fuel pits and filled up.

As we taxied out after our hour-and-a-half stop in Beirut, we got a little bit of information about the passengers. They were doing okay, all things considered. We learned later that 19 women and children had been released, sliding out of the forward door.

The flight from Beirut to Algeria was somewhat uneventful, except the hijackers continually looked for us to trick them. They feared that every time we talked with each other we were conspiring against them. That was, of course, on our minds; but in reality we were too busy for any elaborate plans. Our first concern was to get the airplane back on the ground; we didn't want anything to go wrong. We hoped that if we could just get the hijackers to Algeria, they would make their speeches and demands, seek asylum, leave the airplane, and denounce the world or whatever country they wanted. (At this point, we weren't really sure of what they were demanding; everything had been shouted in Arabic.) We just prayed that they would be content to leave the airplane and that the passengers would be safe.

During this first trip to Algeria, however, the passengers were not safe. It was on this leg of our journey that the beatings began. Having identified the military people on board, the hijackers brought forward Kurt Carlson, a major in the Army Reserve, as the first one to beat severely. They tore the armrest off my seat and used it to club him heavily, leaving him slumped on the floor in the cockpit door. Then, on the ground in Algiers, they dragged him back into a seat, probably trying to set an example for the other passengers that they were serious about their "mission." It had its effect.

This four-hour flight from Beirut to Algiers took us first past Cyprus, then Crete. We then had a long stretch of open sea until Malta. Soon thereafter, Tunisia radioed that we did not have permission to fly in their air space. We demonstrated on the map to the hijackers that we would center our route northwest between Sicily and Tunisia and then turn back a little more straight west for Algiers.

About 100 miles out of Algiers, the hijackers started making their speeches. Apparently, their demands were voiced at this time. Algiers naturally told us that they were closed and that we could not land. We told them that we were going to land because if we did not, the hijackers would blow up the airplane. (We weren't sure what Algiers would do, but we figured that it couldn't be any worse than being blown up in the air.)

We proceeded and Algiers opened the airport. We taxied down to the end of the runway and stopped, surrounded by the Algerian military. We shut down the engines and awaited further instructions. There was a lot of talk back and forth between the hijackers and the tower—a lot of demands—but we just sat there waiting for the hijackers to tell us what to do.

Apparently, the demands were not being met—so we sat and sat. We had the auxiliary power unit running, with the air conditioners going full force, but with a plane full of people at midday, it got hotter and hotter. Some of the passengers were beginning to suffer from the heat, but there was nothing we could do.

We received sporadic reports from the flight attendants, primarily Uli, about what was going on in the passenger section. And, at about this time, we learned of the hijackers' demands—that the Lebanese hostages in Israel be released.

This is when we all—crew and passengers—first realized that we were hostages and not just hijacked. Now we began to understand that we were pawns—bargaining chips—in some Middle East political situation.

Hostages!

When we realized we were hostages, we felt somewhat safer because the hijackers needed us to make a trade. However, that feeling didn't last long. Because things did not go well, the hijackers became agitated and the beatings intensified.

The beatings caused me to feel a great deal of disrespect toward these people who claimed, in the name of their religion, that they could do this to innocent people. And the anger! I can remember their favorite saying as they were beating on Carlson: "You s-- of a b----! You s-- of a b----!" They repeated this over and over again. And after Carlson, they started on the Navy Seals.

The beatings also caused me a great deal of frustration. Everything inside me said to go to the victim's defense—yet I didn't know how to do it safely. While one hijacker did the beating, the other held a gun or a grenade. It didn't matter if we were on the ground or airborne, we couldn't do anything without them blowing up the airplane. Our only consolation was that the victims were surviving. I did get to glance down where they were slumped, and they looked pretty bad; but I could see that they had not been killed.

Once Before a Hostage

I think back now and wonder what it was that enabled me to feel frustrated and yet, in a calm sort of way, to be deliberate in my actions and to continue with what needed doing. Sometimes I felt guilty about being calm—and I wonder why I was. The only thing I can think of is the stories from my past, about my family and me being held hostage in China during World War II.

My father had been a missionary in Shasi, China, since 1928. When the Japanese overran the country and occupied Shasi in June 1940, they were evidentally cordial enough to us. But after the bombing of Pearl Harbor we were considered prisoners of war. After four months we were moved to Hankow for two months. From there we were shipped on the Yanztze River to Shanghai for three weeks.

I was only about a year-and-a-half to two years old at the time, but my parents and older sisters later told me many stories of what they saw and heard. I heard many times about the atrocities of the Japanese occupational force as it confronted Chinese military people or Chinese sympathizers.

The stories are not pleasant. But I also heard of my family's unwavering trust in God and their prayers to Him to deliver us out of those situations. And He did. On June 29, 1942, we were sent to

Lourenco Marquez, Mozambique, where we were traded for Japanese prisoners of war. From there we sailed around South Africa to Rio de Janeiro and then on to New York, where we arrived on Aug. 25, 1942. My family's stories told not only of their deliverance but of *mine,* not only of the Savior's protection for them but also for *me.*

As the years went by I began to learn more of my parents' God and to trust in Him. I developed a life of trust and prayer. I grew to depend more and more on God for more and more of the activities in my life. The trust grew to maturity. And now, during this crisis, the same trust carried over. It was simply a continuation, although now in a more desperate situation.

There was no great change. There was no sudden turning to God. I merely experienced a transition from life's ordinary situations to a very extraordinary one.

I was grateful for a mature prayer life. Years before, I deliberately had begun to "pray continually" in the manner in which I think Paul was talking in 1 Thess. 5:17. I'm not necessarily formal about it. I don't always open and close my prayers in a formal manner. As I live my life I try to do everything as "working for the Lord" (Col. 3:23) and I talk to Him in an almost conversational way, at any moment, at any time, as I'm doing anything. I seek guidance in just about all the everyday affairs of life.

This was especially helpful to me as we were prevented by the hijackers from talking to anybody. There were many long silences as we just bored along through the sky and as we sat on the ground in Algiers, waiting for them to work out the necessary arrangements. Those were the times I had some very long prayers. I would pray:

> Lord, I know I'm not the only one praying. There are a whole bunch of us on the airplane who are praying. You've promised that where two or three are gathered together, there are You in the midst. Therefore, we know You are in our midst and that anything we ask, in faith, You will grant . . . . No matter what works out, we know it's in Your hands. All things work together for good for them that love You and are called according to Your purpose. I know I've been called or I wouldn't be here talking to You now. Therefore, where is the good in this? How is this going to

work out? What is going to happen? Will we live or die?

In Algiers, the hijackers were very desperate, and we worried that they might try for an alternate "success": suicide. They seemed to believe that this would make them—and Islam—look glorious in the eyes of the world. What a twisted and corrupt teaching that God would be pleased with them blowing up themselves and many innocent people! Surely Satan is behind such thoughts. Nevertheless, we *knew* that God would hear our prayers and we *prayed* that He would deliver us, and we *trusted* that no matter what, He would be with us, even if the hijackers did blow us—and themselves—apart. It was a matter now of praying:

> Well, at any moment something could happen, God. We'll cross that bridge when we come to it. Right now, help us through this moment. Give us the strength and the courage not only to live with this but also to be consistent with the same faith that we've had all these years and to trust that all things are going to work out well. Lay out my path with your strong rocks, and let me walk on them wherever they lead. And give us the wisdom to handle whatever is going to come next.

Believe me, I prayed a great deal for wisdom in words and actions so that we wouldn't do something stupid. We all had begun already to formulate the idea of "maximum survival," of meeting the hijackers' demands in any way that we could, of salvaging the situation without getting anybody hurt. This was not a military situation, so there could be no "acceptable losses." We had hoped that everything would be over when the hijackers got off the plane in Algiers and found asylum.

That hope wasn't to be. Even so, we knew that as each moment passed, God had kept us alive a little longer for some purpose. We didn't know yet what that purpose was going to be or why we were alive right now. But it was important, at least in my eyes, that we remain absolutely consistent in behavior and in trusting faith. It became a disciplined effort, really, in faith and trust to pray simply:

> Okay, Lord, it's in Your hands. We have to trust in You. We've trusted in You all our lives, but it seems a little more

critical at this point. We're not making any change in our trust, just admitting that in this case it is easier to trust in You because there is nothing else we can do. Lord, it's all Yours. What are You going to do with us?

2.

A Hostage World

As time unfolded during the 17 days, particularly after our final landing in Beirut, when the initial hijackers were replaced by guards, we began to perceive that we were not the only hostages. Our new guards as well as the original hijackers were hostages, too. This became evident as we observed their behavior and listened to them discuss their motives.

They were trapped in a civil and religious war that pitted Lebanese against Lebanese. They were afraid for their families. They could do very little without inviting retaliation. Even those older guards who were against violence and who wanted to help us couldn't do so because they were afraid of bringing harm to themselves or their families.

They were hostages, not just of war but of a whole system built around a religious animosity that dragged them into confrontation, chaos, and anarchy. This seemed particularly true about the Shi'ite Muslims, a minority in world Islam, who teach *Jihad* ("exertion") to promote their faith, which results for the Hezbollah (the extremist Shi'ites) in a "holy war" and suicide missions. It was to this group that the hijackers belonged.

To understand why all the Lebanese are hostage, consider their history:

The people of Lebanon belong to a variety of religious groups, the largest of which are the Shi'ite and Sunni Muslims, the Maronite Christians and the Druze. The people of Lebanon often feel more loyalty to their sect than to a unified Lebanon.

From the early 16th century until the end of WWI, Lebanon was part of the Ottoman Empire. The present system of dividing

31

power according to religious affiliation goes back to the Turkish system of allowing each religious group some autonomy as long as its members paid their taxes. After WWI, Lebanon became part of the mandate assigned to France by the League of Nations.

When France granted Lebanon its independence in 1943, a 1932 census was consulted to decide how to organize the government. According to this census the most populous group was the Maronite Christians with the Sunni Muslims having the second largest population. These two groups worked out an agreement called the National Pact, which gave the presidency to a Maronite and the office of prime minister to a Sunni.

In recent years, however, the Shi'ite Muslims have become the predominent population, though they hold little political or economic power. As one of their political goals, many Shi'ites hope to establish an Islamic state similar to Iran—although only the extremist Hezbollah are openly pro-Iranian.

The Amal party, the majority of Shi'ites in Lebanon, seems to have the backing of Syria, which considers Lebanon its protectorate. As we observed members of the Amal, many of them seemed to us to be "Jack-Muslims"—meaning that they didn't observe strictly all the teachings of the Shi'ite faith, although they maintained "membership" because of their heritage.

Currently, the Maronite Christians still remain a strong political force in Lebanon, but a tenuous coalition between the moderate Amal and the Druze threatens the political power of the Christians. How much influence Hezbollah has on the Amal Shi'ites remains to be determined—in part because the size and strength of Hezbollah (as well as other extremist factions) is unknown.

What is known is that each faction in Lebanon is demanding its perceived rights—party against party, and religion against religion. And each is willing to wage war to achieve its ends. Everyone is armed and everyone is now a hostage to violence, to bloodshed, to destruction and death.

In addition to the bondage of internal conflict, Lebanon is often held hostage by outside powers. The Israelis, the Syrians, the Palestine Liberation Organization, the USA and the USSR all have vested interests in what happens in Lebanon. Lacking internal cohesiveness and a unified national will, Lebanon is often unable to resist the influence of these powers, even when that influence is not in Lebanon's best interest.

After the original hijackers had murdered Navy man Robert Stethem, and after militia from both the Amal and Hezbollah parties had boarded the plane, the tensions between the two worked in our favor. For example, when the Hezbollah extremists acted a bit childish, some of the more mature Amal would come to our aid and defend us.

We therefore came to appreciate a few of the Amal and spent time talking together. Although they usually began by condemning a stereotyped America (in order to teach us the "truth"), we would describe to them at length in what ways their ideas were misconceptions and were holding their minds hostage. We ended up being ambassadors for America.

When one particular young man discovered all the booze bottles on the airplane, he launched into a description of America as a center of discos, whiskey, and sex. (After a number of such "discussion starters," we nicknamed him "Disco Ali.") This gave the three of us a chance to teach by example as well as by words. Disco Ali tried to get us to have a drink with him. As this would have been a violation of Islamic law, I don't know whether he would have drunk with us or not. At any rate, we declined. We wanted to maintain our professional standards. As long as we were on the airplane, we felt we were on duty and had to do all we could to maintain the airplane and keep things under control. We also feared that drinking alcohol would confirm his opinions about Americans.

Surprisingly, some of Disco Ali's observations about Americans were gathered during a short stay in the United States, visiting relatives on the East Coast. He observed personally and on American TV that "all" young people in America were oriented to discos, whiskey, and sex. He was quite adamant that this must be how all Americans behave. We enjoyed Disco Ali's company. But his perceptions of America bothered us and saddened us.

Hostages to Self-Centeredness

We thought about our discussions with Disco Ali and others—
and wondered who the image makers in America really are. What's
happening? Are the image makers merely reflecting on reality, or are
their images coming from their own minds and actually helping to
bring down our moral standards? Is this a "chicken versus egg" question? Wherever it started, Disco Ali saw it.

I was struck by the contrast between his image of America and
the image of American life as presented in the films from the 1940s
and early 50s that we later watched with the Amal guards in a fire
station. The movies were pretty "straight." Where is the change coming from? Who's giving the push? And why in this direction?

Could it be that the different moral standard portrayed in those
old movies and Disco Ali's perception of how we behave today is an
indication that we are slowly becoming hostage to the same evil push
and shove as Lebanon—even though in a less warlike, violent way?
Isn't the result the same: self-centered gratification? Whether in Lebanon or America, we are all hostages to self-centeredness.

Hostage to Satan

When we look at the self-centeredness in our society, it is easy
to understand why Disco Ali believes the Ayatollah Khomeini when
he describes America as the great Satan and the Western world as
manifesting all the evil in the world. On the other hand, Khomeini
promotes the twisted truth that it's good to sacrifice human life in
suicide missions that bring about retaliation and further destruction—
which end in either anarchy and chaos or in totalitarianism.

Shi'ite Muslim Iran exists because of an evil teaching disguised
as truth. Real truth rests in God, manifest in Jesus Christ, who brings
harmony, peace, and life instead of disharmony, violence, and death.
He alone is the hope of the world.

He also is the only hope for the West, for we too are confronted
by Satan, although in different terms and forms.

In my experiences in the working world, I deal with many good
people who talk about a vague, universal god. In America we ascribe
to a few of his laws and call ourselves a religious nation. As the god

of every religion, he seems such a simple god to believe in. He can be called by any name. He can be worshiped conveniently in any form all over the world. He makes few demands. And, best of all, he does not convict us of our selfishness and sin.

I discern such a god to be the creation of Satan. He twists the truth that "God requires perfect obedience" into "Because God is love, He does not really require a full accounting for our sins." He re-asks, "Yea, hath God said . . . ?" (Gen. 3:1 KJV). He promises an earthly paradise of self-centered pleasures. He comforts us by telling us that we're not so bad. He assures us that we are okay the way we are. He cautions us not to be so self-righteous that we condemn the faith of other religions, but that we seek out what piece of truth each one has. And since this deceiver is Satan, he leads us to believe we have no need for Jesus, who lived and died to atone for our sins and rose again.

As we are sucked into this trap of a nice, universal religion that everybody can accept but which saves no one, I see a world in bondage to the would-be god of earth: Satan.

Hostages: Hope in the Lord

Our only hope during Flight 847, and in this world, was and is our powerful God in heaven. Even when our situation was at its worst, we knew that it was in God's hands. We could trust in Him just as the patriarchs of the Old Testament had trusted in Him. We could trust in Him that, somehow, all things would work together for some good (Rom. 8:28). Whenever that passage crossed our minds, it reassured us. It quietly reminded us that God was by our side, that He would continue to be with us, and that we need not fear anything. We simply had to wait and see what God would do.

As our hostage situation progressed, the thought occurred over and over again as I studied Scripture: God is in charge. He has not only saved us from eternal death, He is also in charge in all the current, daily events. And while evil things do affect us in this world, nevertheless, in His mercy, He can turn these evil things into good. We saw this as He continued to preserve us in all the things that were necessary. He would not permit us to be tempted beyond our ability to resist, not even the temptation to do things on our own. And situations were created according to His will in such a way that we would see His hand as things worked themselves out.

All in all, we felt comfortable with the direction in which He led us, especially on the last leg of the flight from Algiers to Beirut. Things did seem to come together quite nicely. We did seem to see God leading us in the direction of a solution. And, the further along we went, the more comfortable we felt with what we were doing. We felt good about how He worked things out in Beirut on our last stop, when the airplane couldn't go on and there was no reason for the hijackers to remain on board—which was the first radical change in the sequence of events. And while it seemed that men were working out the political situation, our hope was still in the Lord.

3.

Life on
the Plane

By the afternoon of Monday, June 17, day 4 of the hijacking, all of the passengers had been removed—most of them freed; 37 were still held hostage, scattered around Beirut. Testrake, Maresca, and I remained on board the plane. The tension and anxiety remained. We wondered what was happening to the others. And we wondered what might happen to us.

At the same time, we tried to support each other and to provide for each other's needs. We prayer together. We studied Scripture. (I've never had so much time to study Scripture and to pray.) On Sunday, June 23, day 10 of the hijacking, Testrake and I held a worship service for ourselves.

A lot of our time was spent handling small domestic affairs. We realized that as long as we were on the airplane, we had a responsibility for its ongoing maintenance. We were on duty the whole time we were there.

Those duties included making sure that no damage was done to the airplane. And since we couldn't sit in the cockpit day after day, we spent a great deal of our time in the back. But as soon as we vacated the cockpit, the young guards gravitated to it. They loved it. They acted like high school seniors on a class trip. They played with the equipment, lowered and raised the aft stairs, ran excitedly up and down the aisles, and got excited about anything that came along. They loved to make as much commotion as possible—which included occasionally firing guns out the window to demand more food, cigarettes, or Cokes.

But sitting in the cockpit seemed to make them feel in control of this "pirate booty" they had captured.

They delighted in playing with things. Some of their play was harmless—such as turning the lights on and off at night. Some of their play could have caused serious damage, so we were continually in and out of the cockpit, checking on what they had or hadn't done, trying to keep the systems from being damaged. We deactivated a number of systems so that they wouldn't be harmed. All this required vigilance on our part, but it also gave us a way to maintain control of the operation of the airplane so that it was in our hands and not theirs.

The growing mess in the cockpit was discouraging. Pop would be spilled all over consoles and gauges. Cigarette ashes stuck to everything. Papers and other remnants of their search for booty were all over the floor. And because the guards approached the plane through a field, they tracked mud all over everything. The plane was a mess.

Most nights the plane became our own big red and white camper. We'd retire to the coach section, where the three seats across provided the longest space. We'd raise the arm rests and have some sort of bed—though not too spacious.

Life was not too bad. We could live with most things—except their toilet habits, which were considerably different from ours. Although a clean people, many Middle Easterners are accustomed to squatting over an opening and then washing themselves. Doing this on the plane resulted in a great deal of mud up on the toilet seats and a lot of water floating on the floor. A total mess! We found it intolerable according to our Western bathroom habits.

The lavatories were so bad that we tried to avoid using them. Phil Maresca had a particularly large appetite and was always hungry. But we would remind him, "Phil, you've got to remember that the more food you eat, the more often you're going to have to use the bathroom." The thought rapidly spoiled his appetite.

We had to gain some control over the sanitation. Finally some Middle East Airlines people came on board to clean the airplane, and we explained our dilemma to them. As the solution, we set aside one of the aft lavatories strictly for our use. Sometimes our plan worked and sometimes not.

The first doctor to give those of us on the plane a checkup accused the guards of living in a pig pen. They didn't like hearing that. So, for a while, the lavatory plan worked. But the word didn't always get passed on from shift to shift, and pretty soon the guards would start using our lavatory again. But once we got on top of the job, we were able to keep the lavatories relatively clean. And, surprisingly, the guards soon learned from us how to keep a toilet clean.

Whenever food was brought aboard, the guards tended to mess up everything. After eating, garbage would be spread all over the airplane. Sometimes the leftovers would sit and rot for long periods of time, attracting flies.

Mealtime itself was generally pleasant. We found the local Lebanese food delicious. For these feasts, we would lay down all the seatbacks, spread out the food, and sit around cross-legged. This was fine until our legs went to sleep or we'd get a cramp from sitting on some hard object, such as someone's machine gun.

It seemed that the guards were continuously mislaying their guns. And, whenever a new shift of guards would come on board, we'd have to help the ones leaving find their guns. We'd look under boxes of uneaten food, trays, folded down seats—wherever. It got to be humorous after a while—but it was still a serious situation. Even though we had many opportunities to take weapons, we weren't sure what advantage that would be. A gun battle on board would kill people—and the repercussions for the rest of the hostages could be disasterous. We also knew that negotiations were taking place, and we didn't want to turn the situation into some type of military operation.

There were times we even felt that the guards were testing us. They would leave a gun conveniently at our disposal and walk away, seeing what we would do with it. We wouldn't touch it. We felt that our actions spoke a consistent witness about a God of peace who did not condone war, fighting, and killing.

I believe it paid off—at least humanly. The guards ended up apologetic and sympathetic about the situation we were in, and they were anxious for our release. When we were finally freed, we know that they regarded Americans with a very high degree of esteem. I wonder what they thought of our God.

Part of our early activities included the adventure of finding out what was around the airplane. Not only could we look out the windows in the daytime, but after we had been there a half-dozen days, they took us off one night around midnight and escourted us to the fire station.

There we were able to take a shower and clean up. We even decided to shave every day so that we would keep ourselves ready to go. This had the psychological effect of helping us to be ready for any eventuality. Plus we didn't feel as though we were accepting the situation as it was. We were anticipating that it was going to be resolved at any time on any day.

It was about day 14, Thursday, June 27, that Phil's spider bite (if that's what it was) started becoming infected. A doctor had previously checked it, but it wasn't too bad at that time. Now our growing concern for him was shared by the Muslim guards. They didn't want him to suffer either and were willing—in fact, insistent—upon calling the doctor. He came (of course, with Amal and Hezbollah guards, because he was most likely a Maronite Christian). This time, with the help of the International Red Cross, the guards were persuaded that the bite required more medical attention and that Maresca should go to the hospital. An ambulance soon came—again with some guards— and took Phil to the American hospital.

It was shortly after this, as we were reading newspapers, that John Testrake pointed out that my father had gone home. Strangely, I wasn't bothered—and that bothered me somewhat. I thought, "This is incredible. My father has just died, and it's not really affecting me. Is there something wrong with me?"

The newspapers made it seem that he had the heart attack because I was being held hostage. Yet, somehow, that didn't strike me as too serious. Other than praying about the situation and committing it to the Lord, there was nothing I could really do. I figured that my family was well in control. They are all blessed with a strong faith. Therefore I needn't worry about that any more than I needed to worry about what was developing now for us.

Later I found out the remarkable circumstances: My father had already been in the hospital; the whole family was with him; he did, just hours before he died, get to ordain his grandson; and he was able to die in peace and happiness, trusting in God's care for me. It was truly a remarkable and joyous occasion for the whole family. Perhaps I suspected all that, and maybe that's why I felt no particular uneasiness at the time.

About this time I began to understand what a disciplined trust in God for all things really is. I began to sense a community developing in the United States and all over the world, Christians all bringing to God essentially the same prayer. I thought, "How can God *not* hear these prayers? He hears them. He acknowledges them. And something's going to work out." It was a comforting feeling.

John and I were uncomfortable reading the various newspaper and magazine accounts of the many political activities. The reports left us feeling that there was an incredible stalemate. In fact, John and I decided that we should quit paying so much attention to the news because it kept us on an unpleasant emotional roller coaster. And in a few days I recognized that my emotions only stablized when I got into the Scriptures. All I could do was trust God.

Later, the other hostages also shared that same frustration, and they too arrived at the same conclusion: all we can do is trust God. It wasn't fatalism, however. We were not saying, "Well, I can't do anything, therefore I trust God." It was a matter of feeling tested. Were we strong enough to truly be willing to put ourselves and the problem in the Lord's hands? As I studied Scripture, I always gained a much higher degree of comfort.

Father Jim McLaughlin and I were discussing that very point just before our release when a newsman photographed us with my hand on his shoulder and with him holding his Bible. It's one of my favorite photos. I had rescued his Bible from the debris on the airplane that was to be thrown out and burned. I first saw the photo in a French newspaper with the caption, "Speaking from the heart," which indeed we were. This was the beginning of what I hope will be a continuing friendship.

4.

The Caldron Community

Who were all these people on this airplane, Flight 847?

With the exception of the church group from Algonquin, Ill., most of the passengers getting on the plane at Athens didn't know each other. Within 24 hours of our final stop in Beirut, the last of the 107 passengers to be released had been freed. I doubt many of them got to know one another very well.

Even the 36 passengers held hostage in Beirut for the entire 17 days were a scattered lot of people from different parts of America. Nor could any one of them get to know the other 35 very well. They were divided and subdivided into small groups and dispersed to various safe houses in Beirut. Each group lived in its own little cove of activity, each one having its own unique experiences.

In the usually calm society of middle America, our freedom enables us to live as private individuals. We can pretty much do our own thing. We don't need to get along with many other people because we can function as individuals.

As hostages, however, we had to get along with each other, at least in our little groups. We had to live with each other's tensions and anxieties and help each other through them. We had to interact to provide for one another's basic needs. We had to support each other, comfort each other, and advise each other. And we had to pray for each other.

Our common experience of being hostages, of being in the caldron, tied us together even while existing apart. Most of us were also tied together in an unseen community by our common faith in Christ. We weren't all Christian, but those who weren't were intermingled in the various safe houses with those who were.

47

As we moved about in our daily routines, we also had to get along with our captors—which put us in the strange situation of being members of an alienated community. I remember when, as a SAC (Strategic Air Command) pilot going in and out of Guam during Vietnam, I heard of a Word War II soldier who had returned to Guam to relive some of his experiences there as a prisoner of the Japanese. He too had learned that people have to interact with the community around them, whether captors or not. No man is an island.

So it was with all of us as hostages in Beirut. We had to adjust to the life that was around us. In this caldron of mixed people, all very close to the boiling point of desperation in our desire to leave, no one was sure that we wouldn't be used selectively by some group to exert pressure on others. No one was sure what was coming next. No one was even sure of what was happening to the other groups. We all felt a great deal of anxiety.

We were many groups, yet one community as we worked together. We experienced a remarkable consensus on how we should behave—especially as our actions might affect the lives of the others scattered throughout the city. If we didn't maintain their interests as well as ours, we could have caused a great deal of harm. As a result, our sense of community included even the people we weren't in contact with.

When we were brought together in the school yard on Day 16, all the small pots were dumped into one great caldron. There we discovered that we were a far closer knit community than we had ever dreamed we would become. Even though each of our individual experiences differed somewhat, there was a similarity. We all had been thinking along the same lines, both in our survival techniques in this alien environment and in our spirituality.

Even our prayers had been the same. We had prayed for each other and had supported each other in prayer. And most of what we had prayed for was the same thing: for trust in God to be in charge of the situation and that He would know best how it should be worked out.

Coming together was a remarkable experience. We were no longer alienated from each other as we unconsciously had been when we first came aboard in Athens. People usually think of alienation as a process of people separating from each other. But after we sensed our new community, we realized that we had started off alienated in our private worlds. What happened reflects the same sequence of events in our relationship with God. Born in sin, we are alienated from God and from each other. Only as God reestablishes our relationship with Him through the atonement of Jesus Christ can we experience a relationship, a community, with each other.

So, the alienation we experience initially in our private worlds as well as the alienation experienced as hostages is nothing more than the alienation from God brought about by Adam and Eve in the first place. Only as we are lifted above this by the power of God in Christ are we able to experience harmony with God and to live a sanctified life. Only then are we enabled to rise above the alienation urged on us by the evil forces of the devil, the world, and our flesh.

When we finally were permitted to read newspapers and magazines, we were thrilled to learn that this sense of community had spread beyond the bounds of our Beirut boiling pot—that it spilled over into the entire world, especially into the American Christian communities.

Everyone seemed drawn into this particular event. Everyone had became concerned about the problem and its possible solution. And everyone had us in their prayers. From the accounts I've since heard, it was a remarkable growing experience for the spiritual community across America and the world.

And we wondered what good God could work out of the hijacking!

We thank God, not only for the Christian community but also for human communities. We need each other to console each other, carry each other's burdens, motivate each other, and trust each other. That's community in action—and it's as much a blessing from our Father as the sun and the rain.

In the early days of persecution, the church went underground for survival. Spiritually, those early Christians didn't need to. Their survival from eternal death had been guaranteed already by what Jesus had done. Rather, they went underground to be able to continue to give physical and emotional support as well as spiritual support to each other in the community. What a blessing!

That's what happened in my home community of Cascade, Idaho, and I'm finding out, in the home communities of all the hostages.

The residents of Cascade consistently supported my wife and family, and, in doing so, provided support for each other as well. The people worked with each other to bring about the many local prayer vigils. They volunteered to meet the day-to-day needs of my family—including our house, yard, and dog. They helped my family with its travel plans. It didn't make any difference what would come along, someone volunteered. There was no need to ask twice for anything. I'm even convinced that as the community got together to discuss ways and means of alleviating the crisis, it strengthened the resolve of the government to bring about a solution. Most importantly, the people pulled together in spirit and in their faith in God through Christ in a way that I believe has never before been witnessed in Cascade. Everyone in this community, myself included, grew closer together spiritually as a result of this event in history—a most unusual result from such a tragic event.

Everybody involved called it a remarkable experience. Nobody wants to forget the unifying experience that they've had as a result of this. And I pray to God that nobody does. I know I don't want to forget; it's been one of the most humbling experiences of my life to hear of everything that happened on behalf of my family and myself.

Cascade experienced one more chapter in human history that points to God's wisdom, power, and ability to do what He wills in order to bring His people together. In spite of the differences between denominations, our veiled hearts are lifted when we see evidences of the power of God in the *whole* Christian church on earth.

*   *   *

I wish I could have been in Cascade to see all this—but I was tied up in Beirut (pun intended). Since I wasn't, I've asked Karolyn Plehal, a resident of Cascade, to tell you some of the specifics.

*   *   *

The town was desperate. We had heard from flight attendant Uli Derickson that Christian had been beaten, but we didn't know how severely.

ABC-TV's exclusive interview with the three pilots appeared early in the morning [on Wednesday, June 19, day 6]. I didn't know anything about it. But, walking downtown that morning, a neighbor said he had it on video. "I want it!" I said. So he ran home, got the video, and said I could have it for four hours.

I watched the tape. I was thrilled. I ran to the bank and told the people there. I stopped at the drugstore and said I'd actually seen Christian, and that he was all right, that he had a scar on his forehead, but it looked like he was fine.

Everybody was on cloud nine!

Suddenly all sorts of people started showing up at my house. Word spread like wildfire that I had a video of Christian. People came in droves—strangers—people I didn't even know were suddenly in my house, watching this video of Christian and hugging, thrilled that he was all right.

I went to vacation Bible school that morning, and the teachers were slipping away from their classes to run across the street to my house to see the video.

God had answered our prayers. The community pulled together. I have friends now that I didn't even know before. Some are people to whom I just said hello on the street before. Now we had a wonderful bond.

The prayer vigils were the most fulfilling thing. More than anything, they helped me deal with the whole situation. There were people in this community who were so strong! We all left those prayer vigils uplifted and with a great sense of peace.

The vigils were held at the Community Christian Church and the Lutheran church, but the people were from all the churches. I recognized people whom I knew were Catholic, some from the Assembly of God, Lutherans of course, and then people too whom I suspect don't go to church. It pulled everybody in. I think we all found that since we had nothing to rely on, since there was nothing we could do as individuals to help Christian, we found ourselves having to rely on God—totally, for the first time.

At the prayer vigils in the Lutheran church one man would stand up and say, "We have talked to Melvia [she was in St. Louis at the funeral of Christian's father] and these are the things she wants us to remember to pray about. She wants us to praise God for the things that have gone right." And then he turned it over to us, and we took turns praying out loud. Another man concluded the prayers. Then we sang a couple of songs and left.

The focus of everybody's conversation was Christian and the hostage situation. We all watched television constantly. And everybody wore a yellow ribbon. They were hanging all over the trees and the signs and the buildings and people's homes. A small group of women bought the yellow ribbon and pins, tied the little bows, and passed them around to anyone who wanted one.

When it was learned that Christian was coming home on the Fourth of July, we planned a big celebration at the airport. But there was no way to involve everybody at the airport, so we decided to have a "Welcome Home" at the airport, a parade down Main Street, and a celebration at Cascade City Park on the lake. The tough part was deciding which part of the celebration you wanted to be involved in—the airport, the parade, or the park.

Ray Arnold, the owner of our local flying service and a close friend of Christian, had flown down to Boise to bring the Zimmermans home that evening. Earlier plans had called for Christian to fly with the governor in the state's plane to McCall, 30 miles north of here, and then travel by motorcade to Cascade. But we in Cascade felt that the important thing was to fly Christian home, directly to Cascade. And that's what we did.

There were hundreds of people at the airport and thousands of people at the park, even though our town's population is less than a thousand. It was such a wonderful time because it was also "Thunder Mountain Days," our big Fourth of July celebration—parades, fireworks, races, town barbeques, rodeo competition, and other things. So people who consider themselves locals for that weekend alone or those who have summer cabins and homes in the area felt Christian was just as much a part of their community as the rest of us. They were as thrilled as those of us who see Christian every day.

It was a grand celebration!

5.

Leaning on the Lord

"Lean on the Lord" has long been the motto for my life—but it wasn't always so. Sometime in 1972 my wife, Melvia, became very involved in Bible study. As a lifelong Lutheran that challenged me to keep up with her rather than expose my Biblical stagnation. So I bought a contemporary English translation and began reading.

I discovered exciting things in Genesis, things that I'd never paid attention to before. I knew I was hooked on Scripture when I found myself enjoying the genealogies. Everything I read in Scripture became a thrill.

Though I previously had studied anything and everything to increase my knowledge, I began to truly understand the guidance of God as I read Proverbs, particularly 3:5–7:

> Trust in the Lord with all your heart and lean not on your
> own understanding; in all your ways acknowledge him,
> and he will make your paths straight. Do not be wise in
> your own eyes; fear the Lord and shun evil.

Finally I understood that it was not necessary for me to understand how God did things; I merely needed to trust Him to do them.

From then on, Melvia and I grew constantly in our Bible study and in our prayer life. It was a dramatic breakthrough when we began praying out loud together. Our Bible study and prayer life seemed to go hand in hand from then on.

Some kind of turnaround had occurred. I dislike using the term *crutch* when referring to God, but in this case it was as if I had discovered that spiritually, I had a broken leg. Rather than hobble along, it was a whole lot easier to lean on the Lord.

I think Melvia felt the same. The Lord was at our side, and we were able to hang onto Him, to lean on Him. We needed Him, not just to teach us doctrinal truth, but to lead us down our path through life, including the ordinary decisions. We have found that when we trust in God and lean on the Lord for guidance, even in ordinary decisions, things work out most comfortably. We may end up going in a direction that we ordinarily wouldn't have taken, but in looking back we can see that the Lord has done the leading. It was a very pleasant experience to know and see that God was involved in our everyday lives.

Leaning on the Lord Aboard Flight 847

Trusting God to guide our paths, to be with us and never leave us or forsake us—all this became very important when the hijacking occurred. Although the first two fanatical Hezbollah members seemed to hold our lives in their hands, I knew that God would work things out and that I could trust Him to work out everything according to what He knew was best for us. It was clear to us that the almighty God of the universe controlled the situation. Whether we lived or died, the Lord's hand surrounded us. This is the nature of the God who reveals Himself to us in Scripture.

That trust sustained us, especially during the first few days when we couldn't talk much. Later, as the plane sat on the ground in Beirut, John Testrake and I discussed this many times. We were amazed by our trust and by the fact that He put us together to support each other.

Actually, I wasn't scheduled to be on Flight 847. The pilot who was assigned had already flown three flights in the area and had requested time off for personal business. Since I hadn't flown my third flight yet, I was assigned to fill in.

In addition, this wasn't the flight the hijackers really wanted. They had planned to commandeer the Athens to New York flight that had been cancelled.

To my mind, I'd have to be blind not to see the hand of the Lord in all this. He knew what evil was about to take place, and He was already working to bring His good out of it. And good it was to be together with such a strong Christian as John.What a wonderful fellowship we had thinking the same thoughts, leaning on the Lord in the same way!

We were surprised by the number of small events that in and of themselves didn't seem very earth-moving; yet as time moved on turned out to be very important. For example, when Uli Derickson was assigned to this flight, who but God could have known we would need someone who spoke German fluently?

Also, when we were enroute on the last leg back to Beirut, and the hijackers intended to go to Yemen or Tehran, someone from TWA convinced U.S. officials to let us on the plane make the final decision. Our choice to land at Beirut, ostensibly for fuel to get to Yeman or Tehran, proved to be part of God's plan for our release.

The Lord provided us tension-breaking moments so that we could survive all of this emotionally. The first time in Algiers, when we were trying to obtain fuel, the airport demanded a credit card— a Shell credit card specifically. It was so ludicrous that it broke us up. Consider the incongruity: The hijackers are waving around loaded guns and grenades with pins pulled; political speeches are being shouted over the radio; pandemonium is everywhere—and the air-port solemnly asks for a Shell credit card. The hijackers couldn't understand why we were laughing—and that made it seem all the more ridiculous.

The Lord also provided us moments to "reach out and touch someone" in gentle but personal ways. For example, remember the girl who had been vacationing in Greece and whom I had greeted as she boarded the airplane at Athens? At one point in Algiers, she walked past me on the grounded plane and repeated, "I'd sure rather be on that beach again."

We needed these little tension breakers. When we were on the ground in Beirut for the long haul, helping the guards find their mis-placed weapons provided such moments.

It was almost funny when the guards discovered how to use the public address system. At first they used it to "broadcast" Arabic music from their portable radios for our pleasure—but that got very old about midnight when they went on and on. Some of the guards began singing songs over the address system—even duets. We were also amused when they discovered how to turn on all the lights inside the plane. Again, that got old when it kept us from sleeping as they ran up and down the aisles.

As Testrake and I later reflected on what God was doing, we realized that these antics of the guards not only provided tension breaks for us, but they also forced us to figure out ways to deactivate the critical systems of the airplane. The process kept us mentally alert—another one of the seemingly minor processes that God was using to work *all* things for good.

A few times during the latter days in Beirut, we were taken off the plane around midnight to shower at the fire station. While there we visited with some well-educated and articulate Amal officers— along with catching glimpses of old, clean, U.S. movies devoid of vulgarities and violence. From what we learned later, at least some of the other hostages had the same or similar experiences. Although it may not seem very significant, we saw the Lord's hand providing all this, allowing everyone to maintain sanity and to feel that the Lord was indeed sustaining them, preserving them, and hearing their prayers.

Leaning on the Lord for the Passengers

While the three of us in the cockpit were able to support each other, we were not sure what was going on with the passengers. We were praying for them, and we knew that the whole world would be praying for them, but we were surprised that people in Beirut were too. At one point, several Middle East Airlines pilots came on board (under guard) to help us in any way they could, and they mentioned that they were praying for all of us. Most likely these pilots were Maronite Christians. We never found out for sure.

It wasn't until we were finally united with the other hostages in the school yard that we had the opportunity to talk to them and find out what they had been doing and how their faith had been holding them up.

Shortly after I got to the school yard, two men from Stethem's diving team came up to let me know that I didn't need to worry about Stethem. They knew him to be a committed Christian. [The *Pentacostal Evangel* has reported since that he became a Christian about a year before and attended the Word of Life Assembly of God church in Springfield, Va.] Though others might not see this as significant, I praise God that Robert Stethem was strong in the Lord and had already been rescued by Him.

Perhaps more than at any other time, I needed to lean on the Lord when Stethem was murdered. He had been thoroughly beaten by the hijackers and was slumped on the floor in the entryway when the frustration and desperation of the hijackers reached a peak. We in the cockpit heard his execution. I've never been near someone being executed. I had never before heard the breath of life going out of a person. It was a surreal experience. I felt totally helpless, afraid. "What is coming next?" I thought. "Is this the beginning of the execution of many? How could I have prevented this? . . . It wasn't me; I'm still alive."

I thanked God for what Stetham's friends told me; my faith was strengthened by knowing this. We continue to hurt for his family, but we know that their loss is their son's gain.

As we talked to others in the school yard, comments concerning praying and trusting in God kept arising. And at this point a lot of thanksgiving was expressed, too, because our release seemed eminent. It was a rather joyous "family reunion." And family we were—to some extent because of our common experiences, but mostly because of our common bond in Jesus Christ, in prayer, and in trust in God. It was particularly refreshing to hear the Algonquin, Ill., church group speak of what a faith-strengthening experience this was for all of them. They had toured the Holy Land and walked where Jesus walked, both on dusty paths in Israel and now through the valley of the shadow of death. There were a lot of spiritual leaders in this operation.

That day in the school yard was an emotional high for everyone. We were all in a celebrating mood, even the Amal guards who rejoiced with us. No Hezbollah were present. It was just like a big party—though we were concerned about getting those last four hostages away from Hezbollah.

At first, we rejoiced in small groups and in one-to-one conversations, talking about our wonderful, loving God.

As the day dragged on, waiting for the last four, we started to entertain ourselves. For example, when a "sheik" came into the school yard and strode very dramatically back and forth with his hands behind his back, talking to one of the Amal leaders, the Catholic priests and I joked that his "vestments" were particularly well-fashioned. We wondered who his tailor was—or whether he had purchased his gown from an American vestment manufacturer.

Later, one of the guards brought a motorcycle into the school yard and sometimes one, two, or three people would do wheelies through the compound. We weren't really in the mood for this much noise, but at least the Amal were entertained. And, I suppose, we were a bit, too. It beat watching the ants.

We finally had to split up again to be taken to safe houses for the night, where we awaited the conclusion of negotiations for the last four hostages. But this time we split up with a new awareness of how God was working in all of this and that while we had been patiently leaning on Him, He was bringing about incredible results, things we never dreamed would be possible. We affirmed what God had done in taking Stethem to his home in heaven, but we also reaffirmed all the other ways, big and small, the Lord was working. Obviously, the Lord was to be thanked for working out some intricate details in the hearts and minds of many people.

We knew everybody was praying for us and we were praying for others, for the other hostages, but especially for our families back home. We prayed that they could bear up under this, that this would not cause severe grief or heartache among them, and that they too would lean on the Lord and trust in God to work this out.

Leaning on the Lord for Family

It was emotionally draining for me whenever I thought of my family. Not that I would concern myself with how Melvia was handling things; I was more concerned with the possibility that my children could be permanently deprived of a father. The thought made me sad. Yet I knew that the Lord had all of our best interests in mind— and if that were to be the case, then it would be all right, because the Lord would be handling this problem, too.

I knew Melvia was strong, that she trusted in the same God as I did. I knew she firmly trusted the promise of her two favorite Bible passages, "I will never leave thee nor forsake thee" (Deut. 31:6 and

Heb. 13:5 KJV) and "all things work together for good to them that love God, to them who are called according to His purpose" (Rom. 8:28 KJV). Also, I knew she could raise the family without me. But I didn't like thinking about that.

I was also concerned somewhat about my sisters and their concern for me, since my father had just gone home. I was concerned that I couldn't share their grief with them. Yet even in all of this, I was convinced that we as a family were able to lean on the Lord and trust Him.

This was not just a pious hope, but the promise of the Psalms. They gave me a great deal of strength. Also, as I read the gospels I was struck by Jesus' insistence that we needed faith, and that we can trust in God for anything—even the things that tend to make us sad. He would handle even those. Therefore, I found myself not only expecting Melvia and the children to lean on the Lord (as they had always done), but I found myself even more tenaciously leaning on the Lord—though I had to discipline myself not to stop now just because of my fears.

Leaning on the Lord for Myself

Every day during the captivity, I would study Scripture. Then on the 15th day we were on the ground [day 16], I began marking the days by reading, for example, Psalm 15 on the 15th day, and Psalm 16 on the next day. Since one psalm wasn't very much, I would also read every 10th one thereafter—e.g., on the 15th day, Psalms 15, 25, and 35.

On that first day in the school yard, I was reading Psalm 17 and became particularly interested in verses 8 and 9a: "Keep me as the apple of your eye; hide me in the shadow of your wings from the wicked who assail me."

Later, as I visited with various people, I asked several if they'd like me to read a psalm to them. With their permission I read the whole 27th Psalm. The words that made the most meaningful statement to us at the time were the first three and last two verses:

The Lord is my light and my salvation—whom shall I fear?
The Lord is the stronghold of my life—of whom shall I be
afraid? When evil men advance against me to devour my

flesh, when my enemies and my foes attack me, they will stumble and fall. Though an army besiege me, my heart will not fear; though war break out against me, even then I will be confident . . . . I am still confident of this: I will see the goodness of the Lord in the land of the living. Wait for the Lord; be strong and take heart and wait for the Lord.

That evening, we returned to the safe houses, disappointed that the negotiations for the final four had not proved successful.

The next day, before we regathered in the school yard, we received a surprise visit from a new group of people. They carried no guns; they moved comfortably among the Lebanese, yet their English was distinctly American. They turned out to be Lebanese-American citizens who had come to assist us. Although fellow Americans, according to Lebanese law they are also Lebanese citizens, and they could move about freely in Beirut. They had come on their own to do whatever was necessary or helpful, and to intervene for us with our captors.

They had planned also to negotiate for the last four being held by the Hezbollah. Before they could do so, a phone call was received that initiated a series of frantic activities. We quickly were loaded up in cars and headed back to the school yard, where we were greeted by the four who had been missing the previous day.

Now we were ready to leave the country—except that there were still two groups that hadn't arrived. We waited—and waited—and began to wonder, "Now what?" We were getting a bit tense.

Finally one group showed up. We waited a little longer, got more anxious and at last the one remaining group appeared—which included Raymond Johnson, from the Roman Catholic parish in Algonquin. He seemed emotionally distraught, perhaps because of the letdown the day before, perhaps because of tension in his last safe house, perhaps because of threats, or perhaps because of the delay. Whatever the reason, he made a beeline for me and asked me once again to read the 27th Psalm. It was an emotional thing for me to do because I'm a very emotional person. As I read the psalm, Ray leaned on me and seemed to grow calmer and comforted. However, the TV crew that taped the whole reading seemed embarrassed. I've noticed since that the media in general was embarrassed by the Christian aspects that prevailed.

The next thing we knew, we were being given a quick briefing concerning what would happen next. There was a roll call; we were loaded into the Red Cross vehicles waiting outside the gates; and we knew we were finally being released.

At that moment, the whole 17-day experience seemed like a surreal, intricately planned, irrational play complete with scenery changes. We the actors had carried out our parts, and all of the subplots had now falled into place, woven together for this final act. And all along, God was the director—and knew the ending. It was incredible!

HOSTAGE IN A HOSTAGE WORLD

*ST. LOUIS:
Benjamin Christian Zimmermann
in grade school.*

*CASCADE, ID: Christian's
family at home: (l to r) William
Steven ("Kéké"), Melvia, Benjamin Christian, (front) Eric
Christian ("Kaliki"), (back) Dr
E. C. Zimmermann, and (on
lap) Elizabeth Kahalé.*

*SHASI, HUPEH, CHINA: Shortly before being
repatriated from China, Missionary E. C. Zimmermann's family posed with the city's occupational officer. (L to r): Dr. E. C. Zimmermann,
Dorothy (Mrs. Wood), Elizabeth (Mrs. Lochhaas), Mrs. E. C. (Anna) Zimmermann, Katharine (Mrs. Ellerbrock), an aide, Benjamin
Christian (about 1-1/2), Major Suga, and a
friend, John Mackay.*

*GOWEN AFB, BOISE, ID:
Zimmermann in his uniform as
a Major in the Idaho
Air National Guard.*

*Rev. Zimmermann pastored Our Sav-
ior Congregation from 1980 to 1983.*

NEW YORK CITY: TWA Flight 847 pilots: (l to r) Co-pilot Philip G. Maresca, Captain John L. Testrake, and Flight Engineer B. Christian Zimmermann.

NEW YORK CITY: TWA Flight 847 flight attendants (l to r) Helen Sheahan, Uli Derickson, Hazel Help, and Elizabeth Howes. Not shown: Jody Cox.

BEIRUT, June 14: Some of the first hostages freed by the hijackers run across the tarmac after sliding down an emergency chute.

Exclusive

JOHN TESTRAKE
Pilot TWA Flight 847

BEIRUT, June 19: A gunman stays close to Pilot Testrake during an ABC television news interview at the hijacked plane. This photo was made from a television screen, courtesy of ABC News.

BEIRUT, June 15: Navyman 2d Class Robert Dean Stethem, slain by one of the original two hijackers.

ANDREWS AIR FORCE BASE, MD, June 18: A Navy honor guard carries the coffin of Navy Seal Robert Dean Stethem as it arrives from Beirut.

Dear President Reagan   June 16 1985
    We the undersigned 32 American hostages
aboard flight 847 are writing you freely,
not under duress. We implore you not
to take any direct military action
on our behalf. Please negotiate quickly
our immediate release by convincing
the Israelis to release the 800 Lebonese
prisoners as requested now.

                              Respectfully,

Rev. James W. McLoughlin   Jerome J. Barrera
    Geneva IL.   Memphis, TN
Thomas V.S. Cullins   Jim Hoskins
    Burlington, Vermont   Indianapolis, IN
Claude E Whitmoyer   Peter Hell
    Severn md   Schoolberg, WI
Mark B. Bova (Brad)   Ralf W. Traugott   80 Electra
    Miami, FL   Aur Lunenburg mass We are
Bob Pool Sr - Hutchinson Kansas   Being treated very well!
Bob Pool Jr Hutchinson Kansas
William J. Darras 343-18-8418   Grant Elliott
Bremeton Hts. IL 16188569   Algonquin Illinois 60102
Raymond Johnson 324-16-3003
Aurora Ill 60505   Steve Willett Thibodaux LA
Richard G. Moon 32 Cedarcliff   Jimmy D. Palmer
Rd. Asheville, N.C. 28803   911 W. Lne
                                  Little Rock Ark

BEIRUT, June 16: The letter written by the remaining 32 hostages on board the plane (other than the crew) to President Reagan. Only some of the names are visible. (Nine hostages were being held somewhere else in Beirut.)

BEIRUT: Anti-U.S. demonstrators march along one of Beirut's streets. Note the absence of women and the poster of Ayatollah Khomeini on one of the cars. One of the placards reads, MUSLIMS YOU HAVE THREW (sic) AMERICA [&] ISRAEL OUT OF THE MIDDLE EAST.

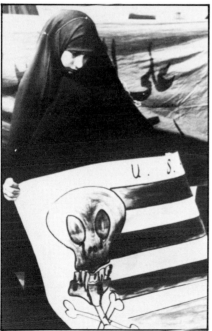

BEIRUT: A young Shi'ite Muslim woman holds a cardboard drawing of an American flag and skull and crossbones with blood dripping from the eyes and teeth during one of the many anti-U.S. rallies held during the hostage crisis.

BEIRUT: Amal militia guard the TWA Boeing 727. (Guards from the Hezbollah party did not wear fatigues.)

BEIRUT: Pilots Testrake and Zimmermann (and Maresca, not shown) were the only three hostages on board the plane from June 17 to June 29, when they joined the others for release.

BEIRUT, June 29: A group of gunmen holding the hijacked plane wave to photographers while the 39 hostages await word of their release—which came the next day.

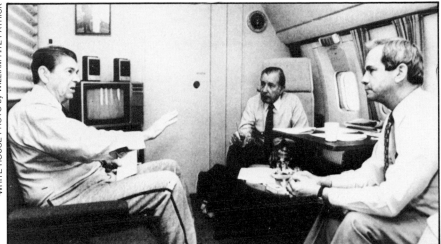

ABOARD AIR FORCE ONE, June 30: President Ronald Reagan, White House Chief of Staff Donald Regan, and National Security Advisor Robert McFarland on route to Dallas discuss the hostage situation.

BEIRUT, June 27: Amal Shi'ite Muslim leader Nabih Berri meets in his home with French Embassy First Secretary Marcel L'uugel to discuss the transfer of the hostages plus two kidnapped Frenchmen to a Western embassy. The plan failed.

BEIRUT, June 30: Hooded Shi'ite Muslims, identified as the two original hijackers of Flight 847, hold a news conference at the Beirut airport terminal that coincided with the release of the hostages to Damascus.

BEIRUT, June 21: Muslims march down one of the city's streets toward the Beirut airport for an anti-U.S. demonstration.

BEIRUT, June 21: Even a young boy holding a poster of the Ayotollah joins the demonstrators amassed at the airport.

BEIRUT, June 21: A human chain protects the truck with the speakers' platform on top at the airport demonstration.

BEIRUT, June 21: One of the original hijackers, still hooded to protect his identity, speaks to the crowd at the airport.

BEIRUT, June 29: Father James Mc-Loughlin clasps his Bible which Christian Zimmermann had rescued from the rubble on the plane. A French newspaper titled this photo "Speaking Heart-to-Heart"—which the two pastors were doing as they waited in vain to be released on this day.

BEIRUT, June 30: An Amal militiaman hands flowers to Co-pilot Maresca as the hostages leave for Damascus. Flowers and fruit were provided for all the hostages.

FRANKFURT, July 1: Pilots Zimmermann and Maresca look on as Captain Testrake is hugged by one of his fellow hostages after their safe arrival at the Rhein-Main Air Force base.

WASHINGTON, D.C., July 2: President and Mrs. Reagan greet Melvia and Christian Zimmermann aboard the L-1011 that brought the hostages from Germany to Andrews Air Force Base.

WASHINGTON, D.C., July 2: After greeting the crew in the Ambassador section of the plane, President and Mrs. Reagan greet the other hostages.

WASHINGTON, D.C., July 2: President and Mrs. Reagan again greet the hostages on the tarmac at Andrews Air Force Base.

NEW YORK CITY, July 3: TWA held a press conference for Zimmermann and the other two pilots before they left for their homes.

ST. LOUIS, July 3: Christian and Melvia Zimmermann are greeted by his sisters, Katharine Ellerbrock (left), of St. Louis, and Dorothy Wood (right), of Salem, MO, at Lambert International Airport. On their way home to Boise, ID, the Zimmermann's stopped in St. Louis to visit his father's grave the next morning at Nashville, IL.

DAVID R. FRAZIER

CASCADE, ID, July 4: Hometown friends greet the Zimmermanns at Cascade's airport after the family flew in via Boise.

DAVID R. FRAZIER

CASCADE, ID, July 4: Cascade's Fourth of July parade featured Christian Zimmermann in a motorcade from the airport to the town's Lake Cascade Park.

LAKE CASCADE PARK, July 4: Christian Zimmermann and son Steve await atop the podium for the ceremonies to begin.

LAKE CASCADE PARK, July 4: Christian's family, as well as the whole town, rejoices to have him home.

"Flight 847 has landed."

6.

The Enemy Identified

After the initial hijackers left the plane, we were guarded by a curious coalition of both Amal Shi'ites and Hezbollah Shi'ites. (At any one time, four Amal and two Hezbollah guards were on board.) Since these members of Hezbollah were not fanatical, we had an opportunity to talk with some of them and listen to their political and religious views.

It soon became apparent that they suffered a tension between what they had been taught by the Ayatollah Khomeini in Iran (their hero and benefactor) and what they were being taught by their political and military leaders in Beirut.

Khomeini taught them that the world should be moving toward an Islamic state—and when it arrived, national borders would cease to exist and there would be world peace. Of course, that meant that Zionist Israel, in the midst of Islam, should be the first to be "converted."

First, however, they needed a unified Islamic Lebanon, free from civil war, in order to direct their efforts against Israel. On the other hand, a unified Lebanon requires pluralism, which they identified as an unacceptable compromise between liberal and ultraliberal Muslims, Druse, and even Maronite Christians. This the Hezbollah couldn't accept. Their hearts and minds—and loyalties—were confused. How could they, Hezbollah, the "Party of God," compromise and still obey Allah's desires as interpreted by Khomeini? The Hezbollah seemed to be caught between fighting other Muslims in Beirut

The principal resource for this chapter is *How to Respond to Islam* by Philip Lochhaas. Copyright © 1981 by Concordia Publishing House.

for purity of doctrine and fighting the "infidels" in Israel (and Israel's ally, the United States).

Where was Islam's promised world peace if Muslims couldn't find it among themselves?

Many Westerners, including Christians, have little or no knowledge of Islam. If anything, we might remember the crusades against the Muslims for control of Jerusalem and the fact that the earlier Muslim expansion toward Europe was halted at the Battle of Tours, France, in A.D. 732.

A more complete and accurate understanding of Islam will help us understand the situation in Lebanon—and the entire Middle East.

What Is Islam and What Is Its Appeal?

First, some terms: *Islam*, the name of the religion, comes from the Arabic word *Aslama*, related to the word for "peace," and connotes that true peace, temporal and eternal, is found by surrendering one's life in obedience to Allah.

Allah is not really a name for God but simply means "God."

Adherents to Islam are called *Muslims,* not Muhammadans. Muhammad, they hold, did not start the religion; he only "transmitted" what Allah had himself begun.

The *Qur'an* (meaning "reading" or "recitation"), the Islamic "Holy Book," was spoken by Allah's angel Gabriel to Muhammad, and must be obeyed. It was written down by Muhammad's followers after his death.

Muhammad and the Development of Islam

Sixth-century Arabia was ripe for a deliverer when Muhammad introduced himself as prophet and preacher of a new faith. Religion, morals, and culture had disintegrated. Drunkenness, gambling, and prostitution filled the land.

At the time Arabia was divided into two distinct regions and cultures. To the south, a stable population of farmers and traders was ruled by the Persians. Northern Arabia was populated by nomadic Bedouin tribes for whom there was no existence apart from the tribe. Because the Bedouin recognized no obligations to anyone outside his own tribe, there were no political or cultural ties to others. Wealthy

Christianized Rome, unified and powerful, controlled most of the trade in Arabia. The Jews were a part of this monopoly. Both Christians and Jews had taken up residence in many of the major Arabian cities.

Religion in both regions of Arabia consisted of the worship of many gods. In the south worship was given to the moon-god and the sun-goddess plus a number of lesser deities. The chief deity of the north was *Allah* (literally, the "God"). The Bedouin of the north, in particular, was intimidated by visions of demonic spirits (Arabic, *jinn*), the terrors of the desert which made their home in sacred rocks and trees.

The date given for Muhammad's birth is A.D. 570; the place was Mecca, a small town on the caravan route between Arabia and Syria. Little is known of Muhammad's childhood and youth beyond the fact that he was raised by relatives after the death of his parents. A great many legends have been attached to his childhood, including mysterious portents at his birth and tales of miracles. Muhammad claimed none of these for himself. It is known that as a youth he entered into service as a merchant for Khadija, a wealthy widow 15 years his senior, whom he later married.

It is highly probably that Muhammad had early contacts with Christians of Syria during his merchant years, for his early preaching reveals some knowledge of Christianity, and the Qur'an contains misconceptions of it. There is, however, no evidence whatsoever of any acceptance of the central doctrines of Christianity; the Trinity, the deity of Christ, His atoning death on the cross, and His resurrection. It is impossible to know whether Muhammad learned only distorted accounts of Biblical events or whether he changed these to conform to his revelations.

At the age of 40, Muhammad proclaimed himself a prophet. Islamic tradition says that the angel Gabriel came to him at the sacred black rock in Mecca with a formal summons to be Allah's messenger.

In a cave in Mount Hira outside of Mecca, Muhammad sought for answers to his spiritual questions. These answers, he reported, came to him in direct revelations as he meditated in solitude.

Angered by the idolatry and immorality around him, Muhammad began preaching consistent monotheism, "There is no God but

'God' (Arabic, *Allah*) and Muhammad is his prophet." Open hostility greeted Muhammad wherever he went, and he was able to gather only a few converts. He comforted himself, however, with the fact that the "earlier prophets," such as Noah, Moses, and Jesus, had also been persecuted.

Town after town rejected Muhammad as he sought to establish himself as Allah's messenger. Finally the little town of Yathrib, which included 60 of his followers, invited him to take up residence. In September A.D. 622, Muhammad arrived in Yathrib. Later the town changed its name to Medina ("the prophet's city") in order to honor Muhammad. Muhammad's move to Medina is called "the Hegira" (Arabic, *Hijra*, "a breaking off from one's own tribe") and today marks the beginning of the Muslim era.

With the Hegira began a period of Muslim expansion. The people of Mecca who had rejected him became Muhammad's enemies, and in the name of Allah he began to prepare a "holy war" against them.

Arming his followers, Muhammed conquered one small village after another and gradually built his strength for an attack on Mecca. In A.D. 630 he entered the city as a conqueror and "purged" the chief shrine of the city of more than 350 deities that were worshiped there. Two years later, having returned to Medina, Muhammad took sick and died on June 8, 632, at the age of 61. By this time he had conquered most of Arabia.

Muhammad's sense of vocation was strong. He appears to have been a passionately religious man with an exceptionally magnetic personality. He made no pretense of infallibility and claimed no miracles for himself, although it would have been common in his culture to do so.

The Qur'an he saw as *the* miracle, something he could not have produced by his own devices. Muhammad believed that it was sent down from heaven into his heart by the angel Gabriel. Although he called himself only the messenger of Allah, he did not hesitate to declare that his coming had been prophesied by Jesus, "who said to the Israelites: 'I am sent forth to you by Allah . . . to give news of an apostle that will come after me whose name is Ahmed [Muhammad].' " Muslim commentators on the Qur'an regard Muhammad also as the fulfillment of those passages of the Bible in which Jesus prophesied the coming of the Counselor to His disciples (John 14:16). Islam teaches that there were true prophets before Muhammad, but he was their culmination. For that reason he is called the "Seal of the Prophets"; no other would come after him.

As a statesman and administrator Muhammad performed brilliantly. Even his enemies conceded that. In spite of the honors that were accorded him in his later years as supreme magistrate, he lived humbly and gave himself in service to his people.

Post-Muhammad Islam

Great confusion followed Muhammad's death. He left no son; hence a power struggle developed over who would be his successor. Ali, one of Muhammad's sons-in-law, became leader of the Muslims in 656, but rivals for his position assassinated him in 661. A Muslim named Mu'awja was made caliph. Ali's followers, however, did not recognize the new caliph, and they made Ali's son Husayn caliph instead. He was killed in 680, but not before his party, Shi'a (or Shi'ite Muslims), became a separate division of Islam. To this day the Shi'ite Party remains distinct from the rest of Islam and considers the "martyrdom" of Husayn of great significance. The Shi'ite Party today constitutes a small minority in Islam but is the dominant party in Iran and Lebanon. It is from the Shi'ite Party that the Ayatollah Khomeini rose to become the leader of Iran.

Muslim armies continued to expand the territory of Islam even while the power struggle was going on, and in the century following Muhammad's death Armenia, Syria, Palestine, Iraq, Persia, Egypt, North Africa, and Spain were conquered. But for the defeat of the Muslim armies advancing from the south at the Battle of Tours, the entire Western world today might be Muslim.

On one hand, as a result of these conquests, primitive countries from Afghanistan westward were united into one great Muslim empire in which medicine, science, and the arts could flourish. Conversely, some highly developed nations such as Persia declined from advanced civilizations into backwardness and poverty.

The Qur'an and Muhammad's Doctrine

Despite the fact that the Qur'an was compiled after Muhammad's death, partly from extant notes and partly from oral tradition, faithful Muslims consider it the very words of Allah, an exact transcript of a book in heaven brought down to Muhammad by Gabriel. It is not to be translated, for to do so would be to destroy the exact quotation of Allah. Translations into other languages are regarded as paraphrases.

The sum of all the Qur'an's teaching is the creed, "There is no God but Allah, and Muhammad is his prophet." It is a platform on which all the sects of Islam can unite.

The Qur'an describes Allah as all-powerful and all-knowing. He does as he pleases. Although he often appears vengeful and sometimes acts arbitrarily, Allah is always described as merciful and compassionate. There is no forgiveness by grace; salvation is associated with right belief and good works. Yet the uncertainty always remains as to what measure of works is acceptable to Allah. This uncertainty was frequently mentioned by the guards on Flight 847. Those whose works are acceptable will enter a paradise of sensuous, blissful experiences. Those whose works are unacceptable will be damned to serve as fuel for the fires of hell. Judgment and retribution were from the outset a major emphasis in Muhammad's preaching. The attitude of the devout Muslim toward the will of Allah is expressed in the name of the religion, *Islam,* "surrender" to Allah.

The Muslim attitude toward the Bible is one of reverence, but all statements of the Bible must be understood as they are interpreted by the Qur'an. "We believe in Allah and that which hath been sent down to us, and that which was sent down to Abraham, and Ishmael, and Isaac, and Jacob, and the tribes, and that which was delivered to Moses, and Jesus, and the prophets from their Lord; we make no distinction between any of them; and to him we are resigned." Thus the Qur'an is believed to confirm the law of Moses and the gospels. Yet there are obvious contradictions. For example, the Qur'an teaches that Jesus was never crucified and that He did not rise from the dead. Muhammad concluded, therefore, that the Bible must have been altered, corrupted in the process of transmission from one generation to another.

No teaching of Christianity has come under more intense attack from Islam than the doctrine of the Trinity. The Qur'an declares unequivocally that Christians worship three gods: God, Jesus, and Mary. Devout Muslims refuse to hear what Christians actually believe about the Triune God. The Qur'an declares that Christians worship three gods, and for the Muslim this is an absolute and infallible revelation.

In denying the deity of Jesus Christ and the truth of His crucifixion and resurrection, Islam has rejected God's saving grace and has turned instead to salvation by the works of the Law. Humanly speaking, Muhammed saw the need for upgrading Arabian society through a unifying law that demanded a moral life. That he achieved—although through it, Satan captured untold millions away from God's saving grace through Christ.

The Five Pillars of Islam

Five demands upon its adherents are made by Islam. There are no substitutes for these. No other works of righteousness are acceptable to Allah unless these first have been satisfied. They are universal throughout all expressions of Islam, are its unifying force and can, in truth, be said to be the "Five Pillars of Islam." They are

1. *The Creed* (Arabic, *Shahada*): "There is no God but Allah, and Muhammad is his prophet." It is mandatory that during his lifetime each Muslim must say this creed at least once correctly and with heartfelt conviction. In practice, however, the devout Muslim speaks it many times a day. In this creed the Muslim not only states his belief, but he sounds forth his evangelistic call to Jew and Christian to turn away from the near "idolatry" of the Torah and the "idolatry" of Christ.

2. *The Ritual Prayer* (Arabic, *Salat*). Prayers are to be said five times daily: upon rising, at noon, midafternoon, after sunset, and before retiring. The prayers consist of set formulas with prescribed bowings and prostration. The prayers serve two purposes in the faith of the Muslim. According to the Qur'an, the most difficult lesson for man to learn is that he is not God; the prayers keep man humble

before Allah. Secondly, the set times for prayer create for the Muslim a sense of participation in a worldwide fellowship.

3. *Almsgiving* (Arabic, *Zakat*). The *required* almsgiving is separate and distinct from voluntary alms, and is set at 1/40 (2 1/2%) of all that a man possesses, that is, his holdings rather than just his income. The Muslim distributes his alms where he sees the most direct need—to debtors unable to meet their obligations, to slaves who are buying their freedom, to transients, and to the desperately needy.

4. *Fasting* (Arabic, *Sawm*). Muslims are required to abstain from food and drink and sexual intercourse from sunrise to sunset during the month of *Ramadan*. Since Islam employs a lunar calendar, the month rotates through all seasons. Such fasting, the Muslim believes, teaches self-discipline and aids in the curbing of appetites also at other times.

5. *The Pilgrimage to Mecca* (Arabic, *Hajj*). It is obligatory for every Muslim during his lifetime to make a pilgrimage to Mecca if he can possibly do so. The pilgrimage includes special ceremonies enroute and a visit to Muhammad's tomb at Medina. The purpose of the pilgrimage is said to be a reminder of the equality of all men and the devotion that all owe to Allah.

Other Muslim Rules

In addition to the "Five Pillars of Islam," rules and prohibitions have been developed to govern all aspects of Muslim life. Where the Qur'an has failed to give specific answers to questions of conduct, Muslims have turned to traditions of Muhammad's oral teachings and personal practices. Because of conflicts among the thousands of traditions, recognized scholars (Arabic, *Mujtahids*) are considered authorized interpreters of a vast and intricate set of laws that govern every human activity. The *mujtahids* are trusted to issue new decrees and interpretations of laws according to changing circumstances.

There is no real ministry or priesthood in Islam. A teacher (Arabic, *Imam*) leads the prayers that are said in the mosques in order that they may be said in unison. On Fridays the *Imam* may also recite a portion of the Qur'an or make application of it to his hearers in a mosque.

Circumcision is not commanded in the Qur'an, but it is observed in all Muslim countries. Pork is regarded as unclean, and there are bans on drinking intoxicating beverages. Liberal Muslims at times interpret the ban on drinking as referring only to drunkenness, but the proscription against gambling remains in full force at all times.

Concerning the role of women, the Qur'an says: "Men have authority over women because Allah has made the one superior to the other and because they spend their wealth to maintain them." The Qur'an also requires the veiling of women. The common interpretation, however, is that Muhammad thought of it as a check on the widespread promiscuity of his day. In the 20th century the practice was abandoned in many Muslin countries. At the order of Khomeini, this practice was reinstated in Iran.

The status of women in Islamic society is a vast improvement over pre-Islamic Arabia, when women had been considered chattel and the killing of girl-babies was common. The Qur'an protects women's rights as citizens and property owners and grants full equality with men in the rights of suffrage and opportunity for education. Although the Qur'an permits Muslim men four legal wives, monogamy is more common today than polygamy.

Islam teaches and practices absolute racial equality, a fact that, no doubt, contributes to its large gains in color-conscious Asia and Africa. However, Muslims are forbidden personal friendships with Christians or Jews, a prohibition that is ignored by many Muslims in foreign lands. The more tolerant Muslims insist that Muhammad granted religious freedom to the people of Medina as a model for all future Muslim states.

The penalty for apostasy from Islam can be harsh. Muslim commentators agree that the Qur'an, chapter 4:89, refers to those who have renounced Islam: "If they desert you, seize them and put them to death wherever you find them." Yet a growing number of Muslim nations accept the United Nations charter, which grants freedom to persons to change their religious beliefs.

Muslim justice can be swift and harsh upon wrongdoers. It allows revenge to the full extent of an injury, such as chopping off the hand of a thief. Most Muslim religious leaders point out that while some crimes are punishable by death according to the Qur'an, in the majority of cases, a lighter punishment is meted out.

Divisions Within Islam

Because all Muslims accept Islam's basic creed and the inviolability of the Qur'an, Islam gives the impression of being a unified belief-system. There are within Islam, however, many sects and conflicting beliefs.

In recent years a nondoctrinal controversy has developed within Islam regarding the extent to which Muslims may become involved in the "Christian" (Western) world. The inability of many Muslims to distinguish between "Christian" and "Western" has led to an intensification of old hatreds and prejudices.

There is much about the West that is attractive to Islamic people. Islam approves initiative and inventiveness and respects the private ownership of property. It accepts profit-making within limits. Muslims may enjoy the good things of life so long as they do not forget their responsibilities to their communities. They have no quarrel with technological advance or industrial expansion, but they object strongly to evils associated with these, such as moral degeneracy and the breakdown of family structure. Muslims are also critical of the racial problems and colonialism they associate with the West.

Complaints of "too much, too fast" are heard in many Muslim lands, where oil exports have brought sudden wealth and new Western influences. To counteract the "corrupting influence of the West," a cry is heard for return to the old standards—strict literal interpretation of the Qur'an and the application of the *Shari'a*, the Muslim religious code of behavior, to civil law.

The Shi'ite Muslims

The vast majority (perhaps 85 percent) of all Muslims in the world adhere to the orthodox, or *Sunnite*, doctrinal position previously described. About 12 percent are *Shi'ite* Muslims, who trace the origin of their party to the death of Muhammad's son-in-law, Ali. The remaining three percent are scattered among several Muslim sects.

Shi'ite Muslims command the attention of the world's news media far out of proportion to their number because they are the ruling majority in Iran, the majority of Lebanon's population, and the most virulently anti-West of all Muslims.

Shi'ites dissent from other Muslims in a number of doctrinal

matters, but the most distinctive difference appears to be the significance attached to the *Imam*. The Imam is a teacher, and there may
be many Imams attached to mosques throughout the Muslim world.
Most Shi'ite Muslims, on the other hand, recognize only exceptional
teachers as Imams and consider them to be illuminated by a spark
of divine light and, therefore, sinless and infallible. These Muslims
have added to the creed of Islam: "There is no God but Allah and
Muhammad is his prophet *and Ali* (the first Imam') *is Allah's confi-
dant.*"

Shi'ite Muslims observe the Five Pillars of Islam and add a Sixth,
Jihad, ("exertion"). Exertion enjoins Muslims to exert themselves to
the utmost to disseminate the Qur'an and make it supreme in the
world. All impediments to the spread of Islam must be removed—
even if through the sword. Yet Iran's seizing of the American embassy
and the capture of Flight 847 have evoked much criticism from both
other Muslim and non-Iranian Shi'ite scholars.

The Shi'ites have divided themselves into a number of parties,
including in Beirut the moderate Amal ("Hope") and the extremist
Hezbollah ("Party of God"), who hold that the one good work that
will guarantee entrance into heaven is dying for Islam. Hence, the
suicide missions. Other cities in Lebanon have their own political
parties. Tripoli, for example includes the Tawheed Islami ("Islam
Unification") and the Syrian-backed Arabian Knights.

Islam and Jesus Christ

In order to understand the Muslim's attitude toward Christ, it
must first be understood that his rejection of Christ is dictated by the
Qur'an and is rooted deep in his belief that Allah created man with
the ability to perform works of righteousness in praise of Allah. In
spite of the fact that, like all men, the Muslim falls short of the righteousness demanded by the Law, he does not admit to the need of
a Savior. Instead, he strives the more for righteousness that he hopes
will be acceptable to Allah.

Scripture opposes this in many places. As one example, John
writes in his first epistle, "This is love: not that we loved God, but
that he loved us and sent his Son as an atoning sacrifice for our sins"
(1 John 4:10).

"What do you think about the Christ? Whose son is He?" (Matt. 22:42). Upon the answer to this question hangs the eternal destiny of every human being. The answer to this question irreconcilably divides Christian and Muslim. There is only one answer: "Anyone who believes in the Son of God has this testimony in his heart. Anyone who does not believe God has made him out to be a liar, because he has not believed the testimony God has given about his Son. And this is the testimony: God has given us eternal life, and this life is in his Son" (1 John 5:10-11).

Yet the Qur'an declares: "Say, We believe in Allah and what is revealed to us; in that which was revealed to Abraham and Ishmael, to Isaac and Jacob and the tribes; and in that which Allah gave Moses and Jesus and the prophets. We discriminate against none of them."

In spite of these claims that the Qur'an confirms the revelation of God in the Bible, it rejects what the Bible teaches concerning Jesus' deity, crucifixion, and resurrection, and the doctrine of the Atonement.

It must be remembered that the culture into which Muhammad was born was filled with the worship of many gods and goddesses, lesser deities, and demons. Muhammad found nothing more repugnant than the superstition and polytheism around him. His early preaching was filled with stern judgment upon all who worshiped more than one God. The sin of associating anything with God as a co-deity, he made plain, was the most deadly of all sins. He included Christians in his denunciation of idolaters, for in his misunderstanding of the Christian religion he supposed that Christians worship three gods—God, Jesus, and Mary. If he could conceive of any sin worse than worshiping more than one God, Muhammad felt that it was believing that God physically fathered a son. The denial of the deity of Christ began with Muhammad's mistaken assumptions about what Christians believe, and in his preaching it grew into an all-out attack on the Christian faith.

Apart from that, the Qur'an has much praise for Jesus. It stresses His sinlessness. It speaks of Him as the "Word of Allah," "the messiah," and "illustrious in this world and the next." In many ways, Muslims have a higher respect for Jesus than some so-called Christians, who look at Jesus as only a gifted teacher and exemplar otherwise no different from themselves. The Qur'an nowhere, however, acknowledges Jesus' deity nor His preexistence from eternity. The Qur'an states: "Jesus was no more than a mortal whom [Allah] favored and made an example to the Israelites."

Jesus' chief significance to Islam lies in the Qur'an's assertion that Jesus prophesied: "An apostle will come after me whose name is Ahmad," a name by which Muhammad is also known in the Qur'an.

Approximately one-third of the words of the Christian gospels are recorded eyewitness accounts of the crucifixion and resurrection of Jesus and events associated with these accounts. The crucifixion is not only central to the New Testament, it is the focus of Old Testament prophecy. Without the crucifixion, there is no forgiveness for man's sins and no hope of eternal life. The apostle Paul, therefore, declared in various forms, "Christ died for our sins according to the Scriptures" (1 Cor. 15:3). Jesus revealed by explicit prophecy that He would be crucified and rise again (Matt. 16:21) and gave His sacrifice for the sins of the world as the purpose of His coming into the world (Mark 10:45).

In a few words the Qur'an dismisses as error the words of Jesus, the evangelists, and the apostles: "[The Jews] have said, Verily we have slain Christ Jesus the son of Mary, the apostle of Allah; yet they slew him not, neither crucified him, but he was represented by one in his likeness . . . . They did not really kill him; but Allah took him up into himself." Most approved Muslim commentaries set forth the common Muslim belief that Allah changed Jesus' features so that those who wanted to crucify Him would not recognize Him. Then Allah raised Him to heaven before He could be seized. Judas, instead, was crucified, so cleverly disguised as Jesus that even Mary and the disciples were deceived. A few commentaries suggest that it was Simon of Cyrene who was crucified, but all agree that it was not Jesus. However, Muslim traditions teach that Jesus will someday descend from paradise, live on earth for about 40 years, become a Muslim, marry and beget children, try once more to call all men to Islam, and then die. He is seen as both being judged by Allah and participating in the judgment.

Without faith in the substitutionary death of the Son of God for the sins of the world (the Atonement), the Muslim must rely on the will of Allah and the faithful performance of the duties of the Five (or Six) Pillars to offset his sins and make him acceptable to Allah. Although each section of the Qur'an begins by naming Allah "the Merciful," the Muslim can only *hope* that Allah will have mercy on him and take him to paradise when he dies. He has no assurance that his works have been performed properly or are sufficient, for in the Qur'an he is constantly reminded that even his actions are shaped by Allah's sovereign decree: "Allah will lead into error whom he pleaseth, and whom he pleaseth he will put in the right way," and "None can guide those whom Allah has led astray. They shall be punished in this life; but more painful is the punishment of the life to come."

In Islam it would be considered an insult to Allah's righteousness and omnipotence to say that Allah "loved the world" or saves man "by grace." To the Muslim, that would imply that Allah was moved or affected by the sinner's lost condition—and that would be contrary to his divine justice.

Yet such is the nature of God as He has revealed Himself in Jesus Christ. He regards with pity man's futile striving for righteousness that will save him. In His grace God does that which only God can do—He satisfies divine justice in man's place. He lifts the uncertainty from man's heart with the free gift of salvation in Jesus Christ: "For God so loved the world that he gave his one and only Son, that whoever believes in him shall not perish but have eternal life. For God did not send his Son into the world to condemn the world, but to save the world through him" (John 3:16-17).

The Enemy Exposed

Considering Satan's reputation as a great deceiver, Islam as well as all religions of the world outside of Christianity are twistings of God's revealed truth. They are developed and polished over the years and certainly attract many great followings. Satan has designed them to appeal to man's fallen nature in conforming God to man's imagination and to his desire to save himself.

The two original hijackers were reflections of what they had been taught; they were not merely a couple of criminal crazies. They were fairly accurate manifestations of the havoc Satan can work in people's lives.

As we looked around Beirut, we could see the manifestation of Satan's influence. What has been happening in Beirut for the last 11 years has been violence, chaos, bloodshed, civil war, and death.

We have seen the enemy, and he is Satan.

7.

The Enemy Confronted

One has to keep in mind that although Satan is the ultimate enemy on earth, neither the original hijackers nor our guards were Satan. They were humans like anyone else, with hopes and dreams, hurts, and frustration, living in a world for which Christ died. The enemy we confronted was Satan's Big Lie: the confusion of his view of the world with truth. This was apparent as he twisted both the truth of God as well as human truths.

For example, Satan had led the original hijackers to rationalize their actions as just. They hijacked an American airplane because they had been taught (and believed) that America was the great Satan, that its government hated Muslims, and that it was using Israel to eliminate them. The Lebanese held hostage by Israel "proved" that to them, and the hijackers wanted that rectified—right now. (That need for immediacy seemed to be part of their basic personality. Even though they might take an hour or two figuring out what they needed, once they did, they needed it "right now." Their fanatical impatience allowed no room even for common sense.) Understanding international politics and lobbying techniques were beyond their Hezbollah view of life. America was simply the great Satan and controlled all of this.

Curiously, both the original hijackers and the guards liked the American people. It was our government, they felt, that legalistically controlled everything. That's true in a religious state such as Iran. It fit what they had been taught by their Hezbollah leaders, and so it must be true about America. If true, then why not fight a hatred toward Muslims with a hatred of the America government?

Many conversations with the hijackers and subsequent Muslim guards (at least the younger ones) began with, "Reagan no good.

85

American government no good. New Jersey no good. American people are good." (We couldn't understand what was wrong with the State of New Jersey—until we later figured out that they were talking about the battleship *New Jersey,* which had shelled part of Beirut in an earlier confrontation.) The phrases came up so frequently from so many different young Muslims that we figured they were taught these few phrases, because they knew very little English otherwise.

I should moderate the above. The older guards, mostly of the Amal party, are not attempting to overthrow their government but to reform it. Nor do they believe in suicide missions—even though they are Shi'ites. Nor did they think that all their country's problems during the past 11 years could be blamed on Reagan and the *New Jersey;* they had lived too long for such naiveté. They remembered the past, peaceful relations with the United States and Beirut's prosperity as an international resort. When they explained this to the young Hezbollah guards, it confused them. Iran's Khomeini had told them that all of their problems were because of Reagan and the American government. That has been pounded into them so deeply that they can't recognize the very obvious possibility that the Ayatollah's ranting concerning the great Satan America are nothing more than a determined effort to cover up Satan himself at work within Islam.

One other word of moderation. While we as Christians cannot accept Islam, we love the Muslim people so much that we want to bring them to a saving knowledge of the true God manifest in Jesus Christ.

Confronting Evil with the Truth

Occasionally, as I sat in my row of seats reading my Bible, a guard would stop by and ask, "Is that your Holy Book?"

"Yes," I would reply.

"Is it true that your Book is written by many people?"

"Yes, my Book is written by many people. God used these people throughout history to testify to His interaction with humans throughout history."

"Oh, but our Holy Book is written by one person because we have one God."

"Yes," I would say. "We believe in one God also." They would respond, "Yes, but our God is greater. We cannot lose. We will always win."

And the first thing that went through my mind was, "What kind of winning are they talking about?" As I looked around at the death and destruction in Beirut, I would ask, "Why is it that if you always win, you're always fighting? You tell us you like the American people, that you love all people, and that you wish to kill no one. Yet as I look around, I see violence and destruction and death. But Jesus teaches love, peace, and life. My God does not teach that the way to peace is through fighting and killing."

At other times they would start the conversation by telling us what they assumed to be correct about Christianity. "Your Jesus was unsuccessful. He did not accomplish what He was supposed to accomplish as a prophet. And in fact, one of His disciples died on the cross, not Him. He went off someplace and got married, had children, and raised a family—and we can show you His grave."

I responded that in those days many people had the name Jesus and, we were sure, they could show us some grave with the name Jesus on it. But they misunderstood the teachings of the New Testament. History, by anyone's standards except the Qur'an, accepts the testimony of witnesses. Many witnesses saw Jesus dying on the cross. That was no disciple who died in His place. Not even the Jews believe that! (This visibly caused them to think.)

Second, those same witnesses and many others observed Him after He rose from the dead. And many of those witnesses themselves died proclaiming what they had seen. That would make no sense at all if they were making up a story. Why would so many die for what they knew to be false? Third, I would ask, "Is Jesus considered by your religion to be a prophet?"

"Yes," they would say, "He was a prophet, but Muhammad was the great prophet who brought everything to a culmination as far as man and God went."

We responded, "How can you respect a prophet who deceived you and told you conflicting things? Muhammad told you that Jesus was a true prophet and you should listen to the prophets. Yet Jesus very clearly taught that He came as the Perfect Lamb to sacrifice

Himself for the sins of all people, including you. He died for all sin so that men wouldn't have to die for their sins, but could live forever. Muhammad told you to listen to this prophet Jesus, but he also told you that what Jesus said wasn't true. How can you follow this deception? Somebody is not telling the truth. Either Jesus is not telling the truth, which makes Him a liar and not a prophet, or your religion is not telling the truth about Him."

This was, I think, the first time they heard anything like this. It may have sounded harsh to them, but since they had first told us what they considered to be true concerning Jesus, we could now correct that untruth.

Our greatest joy, however, came when we could witness to the joy of knowing our sins are forgiven because of Jesus' death and that we don't have to worry whether we've done enough good to merit eternal life.

Curiously enough, they did not debate the issue. Perhaps they had not heard this before. Perhaps they felt unable to grapple with the deeper implications of it. Or, perhaps, they had spent all their lives among other Muslims and had never thought about what Christians really believe.

Or it may be that our guards were practicing the Muslim custom of not insulting a guest by arguing against him.

Confronting Political Evil with Truth

Occasionally, when talking about how they would demonstrate to the world that their God was greater and that they could not lose, the subject of the suicide missions came up.

We'd ask, "Why do you do that?"

"Because it is good for Islam."

"Why is it good for Islam?"

"Because it shows the world that Islam must win and can win; and that our God is stronger."

We told them, "The rest of the world holds Islam in disdain. It brings great shame on Islam when suicide missions kill many innocent people. This type of murder and destruction makes Islam look bad. And, in fact, those involved in such missions are considered to be crazy."

At this they would break into laughter. "We're not crazy. When we kill ourselves in such a suicide mission we go directly to paradise."

And we would say, "Okay; what happens next?"

"Well, of course, the enemy retaliates."

"Who would they retaliate against?"

"Our village," they said. Once the enemy found out where the "suicide heroes" were from, the enemy would retaliate against that place, against their clan.

"That's interesting," we said. "So the enemy won't just roll over and play dead. You believe you have won for Islam, but instead, your home and many of your people—including innocent brothers, sisters, parents, and many friends—will get killed in the retaliation. Is that correct?"

"Yes, that's correct."

"Then, you are telling the world that Islam is to be disdained. You bring about death and destruction; you kill and maim friends, relatives, uncles and aunts, children, and grandparents, and certainly property also—yet they consider you a hero. But you escape by going directly to paradise. It seems to me that your purpose is not for their good nor for the good of Islam, but for yourself. That sounds terribly selfish. You take care of yourself first, and so cause a great deal of damage to your religion's reputation and to the people that you love."

Again, they wouldn't argue with us. We never understood why. Was it that they felt that we would never understand that their relatives, too, would supposedly go directly to paradise?

We observed—and pointed out to our captors—some of the contradictions in their thinking. For example, Hezbollah members (if they listened to the voice of Iran) said that peace would come when Islam prevailed, and that those who obstruct Islam are to be destroyed. Yet they repeatedly told us that they didn't wish to kill anyone. How illogical! The Hezbollah members also believed that Israel should be an Islamic state—and the only way to overcome Israel (and all the enemies of Islam) was to use force. And now that they were armed, this was their desire.

Fortunately, not all Muslims, not even all Shi'ite Muslims, have such a fanatical position. In fact, the Amal people were clear in describing themselves as desiring a democratic, pluralistic government.

As they talked, they sounded very much like Americans—yet they too are historically bound to the Qur'an. How moderate can they remain before being accused of repudiating the "true faith"?

Actually, we wondered how "moderate" even the Hezbollahs were. When they were beating on the passengers during the initial hijacking, they never wanted anyone to watch. Did their conscience bother them? It made us wonder what kind of conscience they had. The hijackers were human beings, but we believed they were captive to a criminal intent.

Confronting Through Actions as Well as Words

At times we were limited in conversational time or by their lack of desire or ability to debate religious issues, so we as individuals could only demonstrate our faith by deliberately avoiding anger, violence, bloodshed, and warfare.

The hijackers as well as the guards had been misinformed for many years by Islamic teachings, not only about America, but also about Christianity. Now we had the opportunity to demonstrate to them by our consistent actions that we were not the way we had been depicted, the way they had been told we would be. They saw us patient in waiting for our God to bring about some result. They saw us, with determination in prayer, trusting in God. They saw us as "long-suffering" in the inconvenience and discomfort of our situation. And they saw us overcome hatred.

One time, a Hezbollah guard, "Fat Ali," was suddenly called off the airplane because his father had been taken to the hospital. (We called him "Fat Ali" because that was his local nickname. We had had many pleasant dealings with him, and he had protected us more than once.) When he returned to the plane, we asked how his father was. He honestly didn't expect us to be concerned about the health of his father. His father wasn't holding us hostage; his parents had nothing to do with us. Why should we be concerned about his father's welfare?

Our guards knew their religion required regular prayer times, facing Mecca. But we never saw them praying for someone else— or reading the Qur'an. Yet they saw us reading our Holy Book—and praying for our enemies in a very informal way. They had never before heard of someone praying for someone else. That was an alien thought to them.

Alienated from God and their fellow man, they had experienced a separation that they knew was there; but, on the basis of their teachings, they didn't know what to do about it. As a result, we observed over the 17 days a softening of their temperament toward us and a willingness to learn from us. Although we were their captives, and they felt they had to teach us about themselves in order to "correct" our supposed hatred of Muslims, everything turned around to the point where they were beginning to observe and study our teachings and behavior.

Similarly, when John Testrake pointed out a newspaper report that my father had died, the guards, to a man, seemed to be very apologetic that this had happened. I think they assumed that the situation had hastened his death. But I explained that he was 88, that he had led a long and happy and joyous life, and that I was happy that he was with God in heaven, with his Lord. They would say, "I'm sorry." But I would explain that there's nothing to be sorry about; he's now with his Lord.

I don't think that's how they expected me to react. I don't think that's how they would have reacted. I didn't blame them for an untimely death. Instead, I took joy in Jesus' promises.

We noticed the Muslims watching what we did. Since it's very difficult to hide feelings, did they seriously observe my reaction to my father's death? If so, they saw my joy in Christ—which I pray caused them to start comparing Muhammad's teachings to Christ's.

Simply Plant the Seed of God's Word

All along, our confrontations were with intelligent people. Many were misled, but that was a manifestation of the work of Satan, not their ability to think. Most of our guards, even the youth, were intelligent. The older people were calmer and more disciplined—but that was to be expected considering their opportunity for education before the civil war and their experiences. It was expected that the younger ones had less education, considering that many schools had not been open for the last eight years or so. But that didn't mean that they were less intelligent.

Whatever their age, I believe we caused them to think in ways that they had never thought before. All we could do was plant the seed of the Gospel—that naturally sinful man has been reconciled to a just God through the substitutionary atonement of God's perfect self in Jesus Christ.

The more we confront the enemy with the teachings of Jesus Christ, the more he retreats.

The enemy has been confronted.

8.

Flight 847 Has Landed

When we were about to leave the Beirut school yard for the second time, we wondered, "Is it really, finally happening?" We were divided into small groups and loaded into vehicles with Red Cross flags on the left rear fenders. We were given flowers and fruit. But then there was a stall. Now what?

I was in a Peugeot with Phil Maresca on my left and Richard Herzberg of Virginia Beach, Va., on my right. We sat there for a long time. The car got so hot we opened the door to let air blow through. Still we waited. Had some new snag come along to complicate the issue? We never were told. Finally the caravan simply started. Curiously, only Amal and Syrian guards accompanied us, no Hezbollah.

As we paraded slowly through the rubbled streets of Beirut, we passed intersection after intersection and row upon row of people. Everybody seemed to be lined up. Everybody was waving. A lot of people tried to shake our hands or at least touch us. Everyone was friendly.

Our stop-and-go parade was just slow enough at first that the press, on foot, could keep up with us. They'd run ahead, stop to take pictures, then run ahead again. As we rolled toward the edge of town, we started picking up speed. Pretty soon we passed the fields on the southern outskirts of town, swung around the airport, and headed east into the mountains.

Traveling through Beirut, we had seen the evidences of war everywhere—pockmarked homes and apartments, buildings blown up, rubble nearly everywhere. Now as we proceeded farther into the hills, we were glad to leave the rubble of the war behind and enjoy the beauty of the country.

We kept moving, next through Druze territory. We knew that as long as we moved, everything was okay—but we weren't out yet. We were still hostages, escorted by various military factions.

As we climbed higher into the mountains and the sun was setting, we welcomed the cooling air. The drive was only 80 miles, but as we went into the night, we started coming upon checkpoints. First Druze checkpoints, then Syrian. We were surprised by the rust color of the Syrian fatigues, but then noticed how well they blended into the red, rust colors of the terrain.

Finally we came to a stop that turned out to be the Syrian border. For some reason we were detained, perhaps to get approval for the Lebanese Amal guards, who insisted on escorting us all the way to the Syrian capital of Damascus. When we asked the Amal what they were going to do after they got there, they said they didn't know; they'd probably spend the night and go back to Beirut the next day.

The highway to Damascus seemed to run six lanes, three each direction. We were able to travel quickly, but at one point the press pulled ahead and turned their cameras, including a very bright light, back on us. I wondered whether this would cause an automobile accident. That's all we needed! Thank God we had a professional driver. All in all, the mood was festive.

Damascus

As we neared Damascus, the hills precluded us from seeing the glow of city lights. Suddenly we were there. We began to feel that we were home, free at last. We had entered a civilized city. The streets were orderly and there was no evidence of war. Condominiums and apartments lined the boulevard as we came into town. We saw people actually obeying traffic signals. And we saw no evidence of any military. What a beautiful contrast to Beirut!

We wound our way through town and soon turned into the Damascus Sheraton. We were greeted by what appeared to be the whole hotel staff in their white uniforms. When we stopped, our Amal guards frantically jumped out and ran up and down past the vehicles, nervously trying to figure out how to remain in control of this situation. All of them had their weapons ready, and several of them carried grenade launchers, making a lot of people nervous with their youthful excitement. No one was prepared for that, and we weren't sure what would happen next. Finally one of the hotel staff came out, armed with nothing more than a small two-way radio, and shooed them out the gate.

In the hotel we were greeted by the American ambassador, William Eagleton, who explained that we would not be spending the night there because the situation was still tense; we weren't yet home free. An American C-141 was sitting on an airport ramp, waiting for us, but a news conference had been arranged first. Ambassador Eagleton reminded us how tenuous the arrangements remained and asked that we not become antagonistic during the news conference. He assured us that we were totally safe, and that cooperative hands were working toward our freedom. We then were led single file into the news conference—which was kept short to avoid the chance of leading questions pushing one of us into saying something that might offend someone.

We left through the kitchen and relaxed for a while, waiting for the two large buses that would take us on the 20-minute ride to the Damascus airport. There, we passed Syrian guards, and the Air Force air crew briefly inspected our bags, loaded us onto the airplane, and we left. Only then did we begin to realize that we truly were on our way. The time was half-past midnight—the end of a long 17th day of being hostages.

Frankfurt

As we landed at Rhein-Main Air Force Base at Frankfurt five-and-a-half hours later, a large cheer went up from all of us. Everyone was excited.

Vice-President Bush came on board to welcome us back to freedom. When we got off the airplane we were cheered by what appeared to be the whole base. Even relatives of some of the ex-hostages were there.

After a couple of brief speeches were made, they loaded us onto buses (after gathering up the stragglers sidetracked by the press) and took us to the military hospital in nearby Wiesbaden. There again we were cheered—by the entire hospital staff. It was nice to see so many people greeting us, but we felt a bit overwhelmed. "This is nothing," we were told; "be prepared for what's waiting for you back home. That's really going to be difficult to comprehend."

At the hospital we were told that we did not have to submit to any checkups; we were civilians, not military, and were free to do as we pleased—even leave the hospital. No one felt like leaving, so the checkups began with the scheduled debriefing, both with medical staff and FBI. I'm sure Simon Grossmayer was grateful for the checkup, for it was then that a spot of skin cancer was detected on his back.

That evening several buses hauled us to the BX, opened especially for us to pick up any travel material we might need. Shopping was easy because TWA picked up the tab.

The next morning, TWA took a vote to see where we wanted to land in the U.S. Everyone wanted to go to New York so they could make immediate connections to other parts of the country. We were shot down by the President's staff on that choice. They insisted that for security reasons we go to Andrews Air Force Base to meet the President.

Washington, D.C., USA

Our chartered Lockheed 1011 took our group (plus those family members who had come to Germany) to Andrews Air Force Base in Washington, D.C. When we landed, I looked out the window and could see a small group of people, mostly our relatives. At the bottom of the stairs I could see my wife, Melvia, along with Testrake's wife. Even a cousin of mine was in the group. Gratefully, all were allowed to come on board. It seemed like such a long time since we had seen each other!

Our reunion was interrupted by a briefing on what would happen next.

The President's helicopter landed and we three pilots and our families were lined up in the ambassador section (behind the first-class section) while the rest of the ex-hostages and their families were in the coach section. The President came on board. I was the first one he met. He introduced his wife, Nancy, and himself, and we thanked him for everything that he had done for us. He was followed by Donald Regan, several other government officials, and (I suppose) his contingency of security guards. Next they met Phil Maresca and finally John Testrake. Then they went into the cabin where President Reagan made a short speech to all of the passengers.

Then the President and his entourage passed back through the ambassador section, through the first-class section (where his Secret Service men were waiting) and down the stairs to the tarmac. Then we went down and again were greeted by the President. The color guard was there, as well as the Air Force band. We proceeded to a roped-off area so we could sit while the President made his address. Then we were free to talk to the press if we liked, or to do anything we wanted.

Finally we "escaped" to a TWA VIP lounge in the airport, where we were able, for the first time, to have a true family get-together. TWA also provided a ticket counter so that we could make arrangements, as we saw fit, to finally fly home.

New York City

Although a number of the ex-hostages arranged to fly out of Washington National, many of us elected to go to Kennedy Airport, New York. TWA had scheduled a press conference for the flight crew that evening, but we canceled it because we were beginning to feel dog-tired. We had had so many enroute debriefings that we were talked out. We wanted time to get better acquainted with some of the passengers and their families and exchange names and addresses.

At New York's Kennedy Airport we were escorted directly to a limousine that took us right downtown to our hotel. We had room service that night, but I found it very difficult to stay awake for the service.

The next morning we felt much better and held a press conference—just us three pilots.

From there Melvia and I went back out to LaGuardia Airport and boarded a flight for Boise, Idaho, via St. Louis, Mo.

St. Louis

In St. Louis we were greeted by a great number of well-wishers—family as well as church people. Police quickly escorted us through the terminal to a small reception area where we met our relatives and representatives from The Lutheran Church—Missouri Synod (our denomination) and from Concordia Seminary. We also had a moment of relaxation with the family—my sisters and their families, and my newly ordained nephew's family (although he had already headed out to Apache, Okla., by that time). How good to exchange hugs and kisses with family!

From there we went into two press conferences with the St. Louis media, which lasted about half an hour. We met privately with some other media people and finally headed for my sister's home in St. Louis.

The visit that evening was important for me because I was able at last to learn what had really happened at my father's passing and at his funeral. He had the joy of ordaining his grandson (my nephew), Keith Ellerbrock, just hours before his passing into eternity. And, when thanked for bringing his family to know Jesus Christ, he had the presence of mind to use his deep understanding of Scripture to say, "No, God came to you." Everything I heard was marvelous.

The Lord's hand distinctly was involved in the events, and He brought them to a very satisfying conclusion. There were no hard feelings. My father died, committing himself and me to the Lord, trusting that the Lord would work out all things. My father died a happy man.

The next morning we went to Nashville, Ill., where my father had been living in retirement. There we got together with some relatives on my mother's side. After breakfast with them, we went to my father's grave. I suppose I needed to see his name on the tomb with my mother's as a catharsis.

Boise

We left St. Louis on a flight to Boise via Salt Lake City. During our layover in Salt Lake City we were interviewed by a few members of the local media.

When we arrived in Boise we really wanted to leave immediately for Cascade, but we agreed to come into the Boise terminal for a brief time.

Boise's welcome was grand, too. My children were there. So too were Idaho's Governor Evans, a lot of friends from Cascade, and friends and coworkers from the Idaho Air National Guard, including General Free, with whom I used to fly F-102s. They all knew we weren't staying there long, yet they came out anyway. It was a great reunion!

After a short visit, my children and niece left with Governor Evans and his wife in one plane, and Melvia and I flew with our close friends from Cascade, Ray and Carol Arnold.

Cascade

We flew in formation to Cascade. As we swung in over the lake, we kept wide so that the governor had plenty of room to land at Cascade's little airport.

Finally I began to feel that I was getting home. Things had been happening rather fast in the last 24 hours and now it was coming to a conclusion

We were greeted instantly by the press. For the first time, the microphones stuck in our faces seemed to distance me from the crowd.

Cascade greeted us with a truly amazing show of love and concern. In front of the hangar a string of people lined up wearing yellow T-shirts, each one with a letter on it spelling "Welcome Home Christian." And what a bunch of smiling faces that turned out to be! We couldn't even say thank you to everyone because there were so many people there.

From the airport we rode in the governor's limousine down Main Street, where another large group of people waited to greet us. What an honor to be the Fourth of July parade! Later, though, I told the sheriff that next year he'd have to find someone else to be the local hero. I could do this only once.

We then drove down to the lakeside park for the public "Welcome Home." There were a lot of speeches, but one comment that meant a lot was one of my own: "TWA Flight 847 has finally landed."

That evening, after Melvia and I were finally in our own home we decided to walk in the dark back to the park to watch the fireworks. The sky was a deep orange at the time. The mountains were silhouetted behind the lake and the fireworks, were in full swing.

Yes, Flight 847 really was over for me.

Is It Really Over?

I wonder. Even though the events of Flight 847 have ended, I think it will have continuing effects on those involved—both in Lebanon and in the U.S. Just as the Lebanese made an impression on us, so we undoubtedly made some kind of impression on them. We hope and pray that there is some heart-moving effect upon the lives and beliefs of those whom we had encountered during out hostage stay in Lebanon.

I know the event had many blessed effects here in Cascade. The community drew closer together. The people prayed together openly. I'm still discovering people here who I never knew were Christians. Certainly this too testifies to the powerful God of the universe and His ability to work things out in incredible ways.

I even met military personnel from all over the world who had been praying for us—and we weren't even from their local communities. Yet because they were Christian, they became a prayer community.

I pray that the Christian momentum doesn't die down. I pray that the spiritual growth that occurred in everyone continues to blossom. It would indeed be tragic if this brief explosion of human interaction would die. I believe the Lord has a better ending designed.

A Fuzzy Ending

The final chapter of this whole episode had a fuzzy, ill-defined ending.

The Lord, of course, began ending it the moment we were first hijacked. But when did we see it? For some it reached a climax as we drove out of that school yard. For others it began to wind down as we came down the hill into Damascus. Or when we arrived at the Damascus hotel. Or when we were greeted by the American ambassador. Or when we got into the C-141, headed for Frankfurt. Or when we landed there on free soil and were met by the Vice-President.

For others of us, who were not yet reunited with our families, the ending had not yet arrived. Some felt the hijacking was over when we touched down at Andrews Air Force Base in Washington, D.C., and the President greeted us. Others felt it only when they finally had the freedom of arranging their own home-bound schedules—and were taking charge of their own lives again.

I began to touch base with reality when I could talk with my sisters about my father's passing and could visit his grave. Then, each step toward Cascade helped me comprehend that I was no longer a hostage in hostile hands, but was now surrounded by friends and family!

Yet, even as I went to bed that first night home, there was a sense of unrealness about all this. As I contemplated what had happened, I also wondered if perhaps, it would never be over. I was home in Cascade; my father was home in heaven. I suppose I won't really be home until I'm home in heaven also.

Is it really over? Not the political implications. Nor, I pray, the spiritual growth evidenced in the lives of so many people. These people have already witnessed to the Gospel of Jesus Christ, the power of God which delivers us from the evil of this world. Now I pray that their witness will continue as a fire throughout all the land until they escape the evil of the world forever and go to be with their Lord.

As we await that time we trust in His promise, "And surely I will be with you always, to the very end of the age" (Matt. 28:20).

9.

Alternate Endings/Futures

Since we've returned home we've heard all sorts of suggestions regarding how the hijacking should have been handled—what the military should have done, what the State Department should have done, how we should retaliate, what the punishment should be, how to prevent it from happening again.

All of the solutions seem to grow out of the frustrated desire that our country must not be walked on again. Seemingly sensible people have suggested that the Sixth Fleet take control of Lebanon (and what a bloodbath that would be!) or at least that we allow the *New Jersey* to pound selected targets. But which targets? We've never precisely identified who "they" are. Another solution suggested: lay down a Napalm carpet across half of Beirut. Or when there was talk of closing down the Beirut airport, some thought we should close it with a bomb. The worst solution—that we plant one gigantic bomb over Beirut and leave a hole in the ground.

The amount of anger and hatred that we would stir by any of these actions would guarantee more bloodshed, more fighting. Nothing would be solved.

The comment has been made that when U.S. property is hijacked, the perpetrators "obviously" have the backing of some government and that, therefore, we (the hostages as well as all Americans) should consider that war has been declared upon us. In that case, the hostages are prisoners of war and should be willing to die for their country—either by trying (in vain) to overpower the hijackers, or by getting killed when a Delta Force attacks. Either way, it would show potential hijackers that their plans won't work and that hijacking is futile. This, supposedly, would stop such an event from ever recurring.

It wouldn't work.

Since the hijackers of TWA 847 were determined to "win," even if it meant blowing up themselves and everyone else with them, then they and their cohorts would have viewed the death of the hostages as a defeat for America. Not only would these "heroes" have blown up all those terrible Americans, they would also have prodded the American government into stupidly giving them an excuse to be martyrs.

Are hostages, in fact, prisoners of war? What if, instead of faraway Muslims, a couple of thieves stopped and robbed a tour bus in Mexico? Would we now consider that war has been declared on America and invade or retaliate against all of Mexico? Of course not.

It's true that someone has to decide how to try and end a situation like this. As hostages, we decided to try for maximum survival. If Delta Force had decided something else, they weren't going to ask our permission—and we knew it. So, in essence, we *were* ready to die; we had no choice in what decisions were being made outside the airplane. We who were inside the plane have since tried to Monday morning quarterback ourselves and we haven't come up with anything that we would do differently.

Based on what we observed, the right choice was made. The people we met, except for the two hijackers, all desired a better, friendly relationship with America. But they don't understand the American government's supposed hatred of Muslims—which is what they perceive to be true based on our support for Israel, on our shelling of Beirut, and on Khomeini's ravings in Iran.

I believe one thing could have been handled better: the press' glorification of suicide missions as proof of "true faith." In most other matters, we were satisfied with the way the press handled things. They were very professional, even to the extent of screening out most sensitive information, though reporters did allow a few things to slip through, perhaps delaying our release by one day.

But I do believe the press could play an instrumental role in reducing terrorism and hijackings. They can show how the hypocrisy of terrorism, supposedly for some god's glory, actually brings death and destruction. Terrorism may achieve a short-term goal, but in the long run it works against the perpetrators' cause. An alert and attentive press could, as a procedural way of doing things, point out the disgrace the hijackers bring to their particular ideology. Any ideology or religion that condones and conducts such deadly criminal and violent activities should be held in disdain and disgust before the rest of the world.

Since Muslims think highly of their religion, I believe that bad press would have the most effect on religiously motivated terrorism. In fact, when Stethem was murdered in Beirut, someone in the control tower radioed to the hijackers, "That's a shame, killing an innocent passenger!" So, I believe bad press would bring more results than mass punishment, which would likely miss the criminals and only cause more hatred while escalating violence.

I also believe that future relationships with Lebanon can be improved if the American public better understands both Islam and its political manifestations in the Middle East. This in no way condones the hijacking. But we do need to rise above the simplistic, bigoted perceptions that so often prevail. In this case a better understanding of the differences between the various Shi'ite Muslim groups and their religo-political positions would have prevented some early misunderstandings. Enhanced cultural and economic relationships promote understanding and thus forstall the need for deadly and violent force in emergencies.

The Future of Christian Witness

There's even a more important reason for learning to understand these people and Islam. If we are to share the love of God in Jesus Christ, we have to do it on a one-to-one basis with the individuals with whom God has put us in touch. We need to understand what makes them tick. How do they think and why? If we offend or antagonize them, or if we show total ignorance concerning how they think and what they believe, then they will never feel comfortable listening to anything we have to say concerning a better way.

Some have asked if I, as a result of this experience, feel a call to be a missionary to the Muslims. I don't—in part because I feel that God already was leading me in another direction, and in part because I don't feel that institutionalized mission work is the most effective method of sharing the Christian faith among Muslims.

Most Islamic countries are moderate and pragmatic concerning the way their religion interacts with politics. Perhaps they have seen too vividly the results of Khomeini's reign in Iran, which has been the source of so much violence, bloodshed, and economic disaster.

I have the feeling that these moderate and pragmatic Muslims would not be totally adverse to a better way. It's possible that they would be receptive to Christianity . . . as the teachings of Jesus. Institutionalized evangelism often comes across as a form of religious colonialism. But if Christianity were brought to Muslims through one-on-one relationships with Christians in the everyday world, comparisons could be made and the legalistic nature of Islam could be exposed. This was my experience on the plane, and from what I observed, was true of the other hostages as well.

Lebanon doesn't need colonialism, but we can offer its people the Lord Jesus to escape their present bondage to evil. This has to be done by the Christian people who live and work with Muslims, Christians who witness as their own cup of God's love and forgiveness bubbles over. However, if we are not submissive to God guiding our lives, if we do not allow God to interact with us through the diligent study of His Word, if we do not commit ourselves to Him in prayer, our cup will never be full, much less run over.

We should not talk of retaliation and vengeance, but rather of forgiveness and hope. As Christians we are to use God's daily blessings consistently to His honor and glory, and to help others also to enjoy God's temporal and eternal blessings. As we interact with people in our individual worlds, we can share that God sent Jesus to die for our sins and so reconciles us to Himself.

Certainly the Muslims need this message. They are hostages to a religion based on their good works that often promotes uncertainty and fear in their relationship to God.

Because we're still sinners we sometimes allow ourselves to remain hostages to our own fear of letting God work in our lives. He has saved us, yet we fear allowing ourselves to live in submission to His will. When we live in fear, we too are hostages. When we lack faith in God's ability to work out all the situations in our life, we are hostages. Even our lack of faith in God's ability to work *through* us reveals that we are hostages to our sinful nature.

Yet we are free because of Jesus the Christ. "While we were still sinners, Christ died for us" (Rom. 5:8), and we are forgiven. This gives us a freedom to work hand-in-hand with our Savior to bring this freedom to anyone and everyone.

God's Spirit working in us conquers our fear of letting Him control our lives. We have freedom, joy, and peace of mind knowing that we are victorious no matter what the circumstances.

We know that we "Traveled with Angels" (TWA) on flight 847 and that we were in God's hands. He was protecting us. We were awed that God worked out everything the way that He did. We wondered at our surprise—for He has promised to work out all things for our good. We were pleased that, with God's strength, no one had to compromise faith, no one had to compromise American loyalty; no one had to compromise principles. Plus, we felt somewhat successful in helping our Muslim captors gain a better understanding of both the American people as well as the role our Christian faith plays in our lives.

One of the pitfalls of witnessing that I have observed in the working world is that so many Christians, especially the more educated, seem to have compartmentalized their lives. To some extent, that's all right; our lives need to be compartmentalized in many areas. But our faith-life should not be. Our faith needs to be the integral, unifying force in our lives. Only with our faith running as a motif through each aspect of our life—whether it be scientific, professional, philosophical, educational, or artistic—only as Almighty God and what He has done for us through Jesus Christ is the basis for every small compartment can we lead a life that allows us to function in a truly healthy sort of way—and so witness to Muslims and the rest of the world.

Trust, Our Continuing Future

In the late 1700s, William Cowper wrote these words for a hymn:

God moves in a mysterious way
His wonders to perform;
He plants His footsteps in the sea
And rides upon the storm.

Judge not the Lord by feeble sense,
But trust Him for His grace;
Behind a frowning providence
Faith sees a smiling face.

Blind unbelief is sure to err
And scan His work in vain;
God is His own interpreter,
And He will make it plain.

You fearful saints, fresh courage take;
The clouds you so much dread
Are big with mercy and will break
In blessing on your head.

"Yes, but . . . " we tend to think. "Just once, Lord, I'd like to know *why*. Why this? Why now? Why me?" Then we start to look for answers that seem at least halfway plausible. Perhaps God allowed this evil so that

—Grossmeyer's cancer would be discovered.

—the moderate Muslims might gain the upper hand in Beirut, and that peace might return.

—pressure will be increased to release the other seven American hostages previously taken in Beirut.

—Cheryl Carlson, the wife of Kurt, would begin a new spiritual life (as she reported happened to her three days after the hijacking began).

—I would be encouraged to move ahead in my ministry with people who could use a retreat center where they could freely talk of, question, and seek out answers to philosophical/religious concerns—a place here in Idaho I'll be calling *L'Abri on Lake Cascade* (a la Francis Schaeffer's L'Abri in Switzerland, which Melvia and I visted recently).

When we look at possible outcomes, we must be careful not to trivialize God by saying that He allows a particular evil event take place *so that* a certain individual good can result (as if God could not find another way), or by assuming that God has a finite limitation to the good He can bring out of any one evil event.

While I don't know enough about the families and lives of the other 38 hostages (much less the original 151), I can comment on my part of the Zimmermann family. How much good did God bring about as a result of our internment in China during World War II? Although I'll never know the complete answer, I can testify to some of the results in the lives of my father's children and grandchildren. As a result of that internment's effect on my life, how many other lives has God touched through mine?

God's good, however we look at it, has a ripple effect.

We hostages were blessed by God's mercy in this situation. But so were many communities across America. Christians came together, first for prayer and then for rejoicing. We cannot ignore the God of the universe, capable of so intricately working out the events that involved the hearts and minds of so many people all over the world, including people who are not in harmony with Him. We cannot ignore Him; nor should we limit Him by our limited minds.

Our mandate is not to understand everything about Him and how He works, but in Jesus Christ to adore Him, love Him, trust Him, and share Him with the world. The God who sent us Jesus has promised, "Never will I leave you; never will I forsake you." So we say with confidence, "The Lord is my helper; I will not be afraid. What can man do to me?" (Heb. 13:5-6).

Appendix A

Biography of B. Christian Zimmermann

Benjamin Christian, the first son (and fourth child) of Dr. E. C. and Anna Zimmermann, was born on April 14, 1940, in Shasi, Hupeh Province, China. Shortly after the bombing of Pearl Harbor, the family was interned for almost seven months and then traded for Japanese prisoners of war on July 23, 1942.

After returning to the United States Christian's family moved to his mother's hometown, Nashville, Ill., while Dr. Zimmermann accepted a call to the new Foreign Mission Training Program at Concordia Seminary, St. Louis, Mo. Dr. Zimmermann commuted from Nashville to St. Louis for three years until the family moved to St. Louis in 1945.

In 1955, Dr. Zimmermann accepted a call to a congregation in Adair, Iowa. While there, Christian (Ben) graduated from Adair High School in 1958. During these years, he developed a love for sports cars and unusual autos. (He still owns the 1960 AC-Ace Bristol in which he and his wife, Melvia, took their honeymoon, and has added a 1955 Chevy Nomad station wagon which they use daily.)

The next year, in 1959, Christian joined the Air Force as part of the last class of active-duty aviation cadets without college degrees to be trained to fly jets. He was assigned to Mountain Home, Idaho, as a Strategic Air Command (SAC) pilot, flying B-47 bombers. During the war in Vietnam, he flew bombers between the U.S. and Guam, supporting a nuclear alert on Guam.

In 1964, while still in the Air Force, Christian met Melvia Pilayo, originally from Waimanalo, Oahu, Hawaii, a stewardess with West Coast Airlines (now called Republic Airlines). They were married in 1965.

Shortly thereafter, Christian transferred to the Idaho Air National Guard. He and Melvia moved to Boise, where he enrolled in what is now Boise State University. He also became a partner in an import auto-parts business in Boise.

In 1968, Christian was hired by TWA. The family moved first to Kansas City, then to the San Francisco Bay area, and then to Boulder Creek, Calif, in the Santa Cruz mountains. Their first son, Eric Christian ("Kaliki"), was born there in 1969. By Christmas, the family moved to Reno, where Christian flew Tactical Air Command RF-101 Voodoos with the Nevada Air National Guard.

In 1971, during a short layoff by TWA, the family moved back to Boise to take a more active role in the auto-parts business. Their second son, William Steven ("Kéké"), was born there in 1973. Soon Christian went back to work for TWA for about a year.

After that year, Christian began to reconsider an old desire: to be in the public ministry. So, at the beginning of summer, 1974, he enrolled at Concordia Seminary. By coincidence, the Zimmermanns were able to purchase the very house in which Christian had lived as a child when his father was a professor at the seminary.

Then, before Christmas of that year, TWA called him back to work.

In spite of the scheduling difficulties, Christian accepted the position with TWA (flying approximately 75 hours a month). He usually flew for TWA on weekends and attended seminary classes during the week.

The Zimmermanns' first daughter, Elizabeth Kahalé, was born in late 1979, just months before Christian's graduation in 1980.

Rev. Zimmermann's first pastoral assignment was to establish a mission in Cascade, Idaho, as an outreach of Our Savior Congregation in McCall, 30 miles north. Christian accepted the assignment as a worker-priest, earning his livelihood with TWA while shepherding the forming group in Cascade. Since he would be working in Cascade, the family purchased a home there, overlooking Lake Cascade. True to form, he rejoined the Idaho Air National Guard (in which he is a Major, now serving as the Headquarters Squadron Commander).

After three years, Christian had accomplished what he had been called to do (establish a mission congregation), and he felt that his public ministry lay in another direction. So, in 1983, he resigned from the call, keeping his position as a pilot for TWA.

Toward the end of 1984 Christian's concern about the way many people compartmentalize religion in their lives led him to consider a noninstitutionalized type of ministry. In February 1985 he and Melvia visited the famous L'Abri Retreat and Study Center in Huemoz, Switzerland, established by Dr. Francis A. Schaeffer. Christian and Melvia examined the retreat center's program and returned to Idaho, confident that this was the style of ministry to which the Lord was leading Christian. With permission to use the name, Christian and Melvia have already begun to make plans for a family ministry, *L'Abri on Lake Cascade,* surrounded by pine and fir, nestled in the majesty of God's mountains.

On Friday, June 14, 1985, while stationed in Athens during his first tour of overseas duty for TWA, his flight was hijacked. He was held hostage till 12:30 am, Monday morning, July 1. He returned home to Cascade on July 4, leaning on the Lord, even more confident that the Lord was leading him to establish L'Abri on Lake Cascade.

Appendix B

Sequence of Events

Flight TWA 847: Athens to Rome

(All Times Local)
NOTE: Takeoff and landing times are quoted as actual lift-off and touchdown times from Zimmermann's log book, transposed from Greenwich Mean Time. They will vary somewhat from times listed in the various media. Various U.S. times are noted when appropriate.

DAY 1: FRIDAY, JUNE 14

9:55a   (12:55a, Cascade, ID)
Lift-off from Athens for Rome. Plane fully loaded at the last moment because a previous, different flight from Athens to New York City had been cancelled and some of those passengers elected to take this flight to Rome and transfer there to NYC. Fuel tanks for Flight 847 hold enough fuel for the original flight plan.

People aboard: 153—
2 hijackers
3 pilots: Captain, Copilot, Flight Engineer Zimmermann
5 attendants (including Purser Mrs. Uli Derickson)
143 passagengers
TOTAL: 151 imminent victims; 2 hijackers

10:10a   (1:10a, Cascade, ID)
Fight 847 hijacked by two Lebanese Hezbollah-Shi'ite Muslims and ordered to Algiers. Due to insufficient fuel, the pilots persuade the hijackers to fly to Beirut for fuel to reach Algiers. To ensure the hijackers' serious intentions, they first pistol-whip Zimmermann, who happens to be closest to the cabin door. The hijackers abuse the 3 cabin crew members off and on for about 1 hour. About 50 minutes later, the hijacking is confirmed, and officials in Washington are notified (1:00a., Washington D.C.).

Beirut Landing 1

11:30a   Ar Beirut for fuel to Algiers.
         19 people (17 women and 2 children) are released.

         Still on board: 3 pilots
         5 cabin attendents 124
         (143-19) passengers
         TOTAL HOSTAGES: 132

         Sometime during this time frame, DELTA FORCE leaves Fort Bragg, NC, for the Mideast.

1:20p   Lv Beirut for Algiers. (A 4-hour flight; but, due to time zone changes, it appears as only 2 hours from east to west and 6 hours from west to east.)

Algiers Landing 1

3:30p (8:30a, Cascade, ID)

Ar Algiers. Hijackers issue demands for the release of 700+ Lebanese captives in Israel in return for the hijacked passengers who are now political hostages. Kurt Carlson, a Major in the Army Reserve, is severly beaten during this time. 21 hostages (mostly women and children) released.

Number of Hostages:
3 pilots on board
5 attendents
103 (124-21) passengers
TOTAL HOSTAGES: 111

8:23p (2:23p, St. Louis, MO)

Lv Algiers for Beirut.

During the day, Christian Zimmermann's father, in a St. Louis hospital, learns of the hijacking.

During the flight, the hijackers talk of "wasting" a crew member in order to gain the support of other Muslims. As the hijackers realize the importance of the crew in order to keep the plane aloft, U.S. military men become the focus of attention.

During the flight, Navy man Stethem happens to become the second focus of the hijackers' extreme criminal violence.

DAY 2, SATURDAY, JUNE 15
Beirut Landing 2

2:20a   (7:20p, Saturday, Walford, MD)
            Ar Beirut.
                    Shortly after landing, Navy man Robert Dean
            Stethem, Walford, MD (who happens to be collapsed at
            the main exit), is executed and dumped on the runway—
            in order to force Amal-Shi'ite Muslims to become involved
            in the hijacking. Navy man Clinton Suggs is marked to
            be the next one killed.
                    Moments later, militiamen from the Muslim Amal
            party (moderate Shi'ites) climb aboard. A Hezbollah
            spokesman also boards the plane.

> **Number of Hostages:**
> 3 pilots on board
> 5 attendants on board
> 102 (103-1) passengers
> TOTAL HOSTAGES: 110

TWA confirms later that "some" more passengers are
removed. These probably are 9 passengers with military
and diplomatic identification, plus one Greek teenager.
They are split into two groups, one of 5 (with the teen)
in a Beirut jail in the Muslim sector, and the other 4.
Evidently the Hezbollah keeps the five as "insurance"
against the Amal, who hold the four.

> **Number of Hostages:**
> 3 pilots on board the plane
> 5 attendants on board the plane
> 93 (102-9) passengers on board the plane
> 9 hostages in a Beirut (5 in jail)
> TOTAL HOSTAGES: 110

4:30a   (8:30p, Saturday, St. Louis, MO)
Keith Ellerbrock, Zimmermann's nephew and his father's grandson, is ordained as a minister at the side of his grandfather's deathbed.

At about the same time (9:30p, Saturday, Waldorf, MD; time approximate) Stethem's body is removed from the runway by the Red Cross.

5:39a   (9:39p, Saturday, St. Louis, MO)
Lv Beirut.

About an hour-and-a-half later, at 11:10p, St. Louis time, Zimmermann's father, the Rev. Dr. Elmer Christian Zimmermann, passes away while the plane is flying somewhere past Greece.

Algiers Landing 2

  7:46a Ar Algiers.

10:00a (Time approximate) A man and daughter plus one woman are released.

> **Number of Hostages:**
> 3 pilots on board
> 5 flight attendants on board
> 90 (93-3) passengers on board
> 9 hostages in Beirut (5 in a jail)
> TOTAL HOSTAGES: 107

Ali Atweh, a hijacker accomplice left in Athens, is flown to Algiers.

  7:00p (Time approximate) Atweh is traded for 51 passengers (mostly Greeks, the five flight attendants, and some additional women and children.

> **Number of Hostages:**
> 3 pilots on board
> 0 (5-5) flight attendants on board
> 44 (90-46) passengers on board
> 9 hostages in Beirut (5 in jail)
> TOTAL HOSTAGES AT THIS TIME: 56

TWA states that there are probably 12 to 15 terrorists now on board.
The three pilots finally get their first chance to sleep.

  8:16p Nine male passengers are seen being released.

> **Number of Hostages:**
> 3 pilots on board
> 35 (44-9) passengers on board
> 9 hostages in Beirut (5 in jail)
> TOTAL HOSTAGES: 47

DAY 3, SUNDAY, JUNE 16

1:45a   3 more male passengers are released.

Number of Hostages now:
3 pilots on board
32 (35-3) passengers on board
9 hostages in Beirut (5 in a jail)
TOTAL HOSTAGES: 44

8:50A   Lv Beirut.

Beirut Landing 3 — and Final Landing

2:50p   Ar Beirut.
During the evening, (around noon, Central Daylight Time) ailing Bob Peel Sr. is released.

Number of Hostages:
3 pilots on board
31 (32-1) passengers on board
9 hostages in Beirut (5 in jail)
TOTAL HOSTAGES: 43

10:32p   Helicopter (Israeli/American?), coming toward Beirut, veers away.

DAY 4, MONDAY, JUNE 17

2:00a   (Time approximate)

During the night, all the passengers are removed from the plane to preclude a commando raid on the plane to free the hostages.

Number of Hostages:
3 pilots on board
40 passengers in Beirut
(5 in jail, 35 in "safe houses")
TOTAL HOSTAGES: 43

2:45p   Berri, the head of the Amal party, releases 3 of the hostages: Greek singer Roussos, his secretary, and the Greek teenager from the jail.

Number of Hostages:
3 pilots on board
37 (40-3) hostages in Beirut (4 in jail, 33 in safe houses)
TOTAL HOSTAGES: 40

Official report: The Amal militia now hold 40 hostages: 3 crew members and 37 passengers. (However, 5 passengers actually are are held by the Hezbollah in a Beirut prison.)

DAY 5, TUESDAY, JUNE 18
DAY 6, WEDNESDAY, JUNE 19
Midmorning. Newsmen are permitted finally to interview the three pilots—who stick their heads out the cockpit window (with a hijacker's gun at their head).

DAY 7, THURSDAY, JUNE 20
7:00p   (11:00a, Nashville, IL, near St. Louis, MO) The Rev. Dr. E. C. Zimmermann, Christian's father, is buried.

8:45p   (Time approximate)
Amal stages a news conference with five of the hostages.

DAY 8, FRIDAY, JUNE 21
For two hours, hundreds of Hezbollahs storm the runway, but the wrong plane.

The Amal confirm that ailing passenger, James Palmer Sr., of Little Rock, Ark., has been seen by a doctor in a Beirut hospital and is now back with his captors.

Three American warships appear off the coast of Lebanon.

12:00n   (3:00a, Cascade, ID)
Zimmermann learns that his father has gone to his eternal home.

DAY 9, SATURDAY, JUNE 22
Amal militia deploy anti-aircraft guns at the airport.

DAY 10, SUNDAY, JUNE 23
Pilots Testrake and Zimmermann conduct a worship service for themselves aboard the plane.

DAY 11, MONDAY, JUNE 24

DAY 12, TUESDAY, JUNE 25

DAY 13, WEDNESDAY, JUNE 26
Ailing passenger James Palmer Sr. is released.

Number of Hostages:
3 pilots aboard the plane
36 (37-1) hostages in Beirut (4 jail, 32 in safe houses)
TOTAL HOSTAGES: 39

DAY 14, THURSDAY, JUNE 27
Pilot Philip Maresca is transferred temporarily to a hospital for treatment for a festering spider bite. He is still being held hostage.

DAY 15, FRIDAY, JUNE 28

The 32 hostages in the safe houses are provided a "farewell dinner" at a hotel near Beirut.

DAY 16, SATURDAY, JUNE 29

The 32 hostages from the safe houses and the three pilots are moved to a Beirut school yard. The four hostages in the jail are not present; the Hezbollah party seems to be using them as a trump card against the Amal. Release negotiations fail, and the 35 people (including the pilots) are returned to safe houses for the night.

DAY 17, SUNDAY, JUNE 30

5:40p   (8:40a, Cascade, ID)

All 39 hostages, reassembled in the school yard, are loaded into cars and motorcaded to Damascus, Syria (about 80 miles away), about a 5-plus hour trip.

During the trip, Christian's nephew (his father's grandson), Rev. Keith Ellerbrock, is installed as pastor in Apache, OK, where it is Sunday morning.

DAY 18, MONDAY, JULY 1

12:30a   (3:30p, Sunday, Cascade, ID)

The plane load of former hostages leaves Damascus for Rhein-Main Air Base (Frankfurt) and the military hospital in Wiesbaden, flying on a USAF C-141.

5:25a   (8:39p, Sunday, Cascade, ID)

Ar Frankfurt.

DAY 19, TUESDAY, JULY 2

1:00p   Lv Frankfurt with 30 of the hostages. The other 9 make separate arrangements.

3:30p   Ar Andrews Air Force Base, Washington, DC.
Many relatives, including Melvia Zimmermann, greet the plane and come aboard. The former hostages are met by Pres. Reagan.
Some of the passengers return home from here.

5:45p   (Time approximate) Lv Washington, DC. Ar Kennedy Airport, New York City about 45 minutes later.

DAY 20, WEDNESDAY, JULY 3

10:00a   TWA press conference.

12:45p   Pilot Christian Zimmermann and family leave for St. Louis.

2:20p   Ar St. Louis, MO.

DAY 21, THURSDAY, JULY 4

9:00a   Zimmermanns visit Christian's father's grave.

12:05p   Lv St. Louis for Cascade, ID, via Boise.

8:30p   Ar home, Cascade, ID.

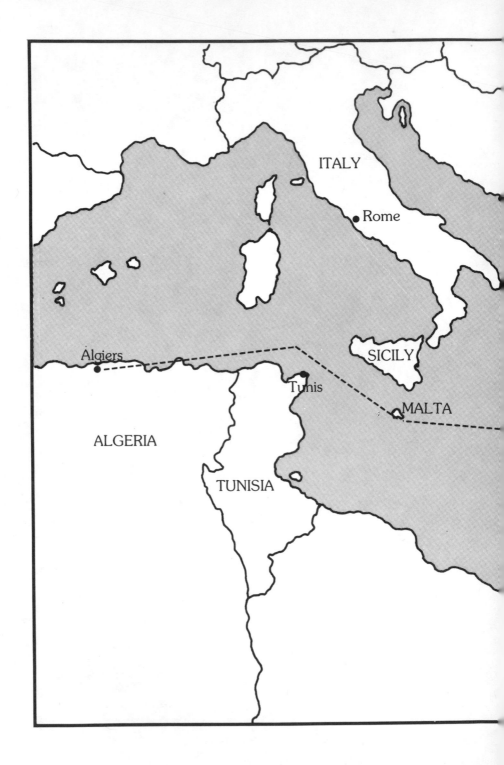

ECE

Athens

CRETE

CYPRUS

SYRIA

LEBANON

Beirut

Damascus

Jerusalem

ISRAEL